U0559275

随着数字产业化和人工智能的迅速发展，信息设计在品牌建设和策划中扮演着至关重要的角色。本书通过丰富的图例进行中西方案例作品的交流，深入研究了品牌策划中的可视化构建、语境和传达。品牌策划可视化设计不仅仅是品牌建设过程中的图形展示，它还得到了多个学科理论的支持。凭借其独特的传播方式，它有助于人们重新构建、理解、记忆和应用品牌信息，并将这一方法发展成为连接认知心理学、人类学研究、市场调研、用户体验研究、数据分析和人工智能研究之间的桥梁。本书旨在展示信息设计助力于品牌在商业、文化和社会领域的应用，以及该领域的前沿发展趋势。

Amid the rapid digital transformation and the growth of artificial intelligence, information design has emerged as a pivotal element in brand development and strategy. In this book, we delve into the intricacies of brand planning, emphasizing the visual construction, contextualization, and communication aspects. Through a wealth of case studies drawn from both eastern and western contexts, we explore how visual design transcends conventional graphic representation in the brand-building process. Supported by theories from diverse disciplines, this unique mode of communication aids in the reconstruction, comprehension, remembering, and application of brand information. It serves as a bridge connecting cognitive psychology, anthropology, market research, user experience studies, data analysis, and artificial intelligence research. Ultimately, this book aims to spotlight information design's role in branding across business, culture, and society within the context of new media, while also highlighting emerging trends in this dynamic field.

INFORMATION
DESIGN & BRANDING

信息设计
与品牌塑造

Photo by Juan Manuel Escalante

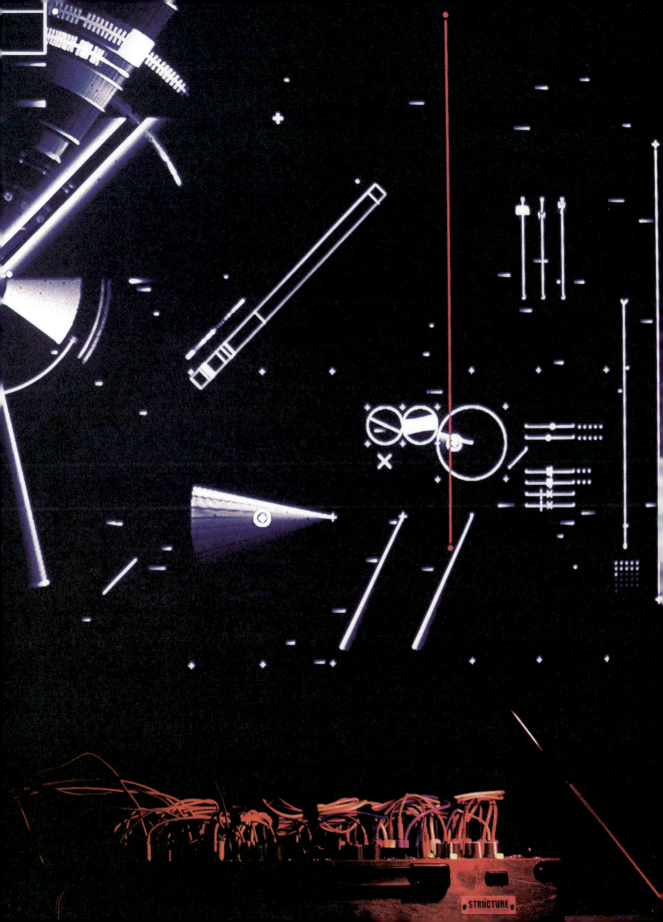

STRUCTURE

INFORMATION
DESIGN & BRANDING

信息设计与品牌塑造

闵洁 王琛 编著

JIE MIN   CHEN WANG

按姓氏的拼音顺序排序
sorted alphabetically by surname

上海文化出版社
SHANGHAI CULTURE PUBLISHING HOUSE

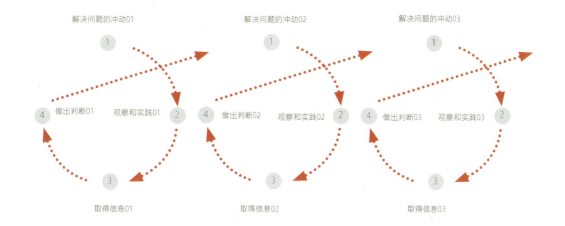

解决问题的冲动01　①　　　　　解决问题的冲动02　①　　　　　解决问题的冲动03　①

④　做出判断01　观察和实践01　②　　④　做出判断02　观察和实践02　②　　④　做出判断03　观察和实践03　②

③　　　　　　　　　　③　　　　　　　　　　③

取得信息01　　　　　　　取得信息02　　　　　　　取得信息03

自我不是现成的，而是通过对行动的选择不断塑造而成。

The self is not something ready-made, but something in continuous formation through choice of action.

约翰·杜威
John Dewey │ philosopher, psychologist │ 1859–1952

A INTRO
概述

B CASE STUDY
实践案例分析

B / 01 实验作品对话

B / 02 文化类

B / 03 互联网类

C INTERVIEW
对话创新设计师

A / 01
信息设计与品牌塑造概述

王琛

模拟化时代 ANALOG TIME		数字化时代 DIGITAL TIME
模拟信号产品	┄┄➤	电子产品和服务行业
建立品牌信任	┄┄➤	用户口碑与回馈
用户接受广告信息	┄┄➤	用户参与品牌共建
打造完美的产品	┄┄➤	产品持续迭代更新
拥有同样的产品	┄┄➤	共享服务及个人订制
关注物质	┄┄➤	关注品牌价值

图1　从模拟时代到数字时代品牌观念的转变

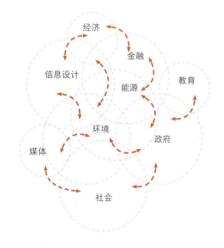

图2　抗解问题（Wicked Problem）

我们目前正亲历着一场信息技术的革命，数字化正深刻地塑造着人类生活的各个层面。20世纪80年代以来，随着模拟化时代向数字化时代的过渡，产品和服务业的形态不断向电子化和智能化转换，数字产品的物理形态进一步消失，而用户与产品交互过程中的体验成为对产品印象的心理印记。同时，用户生成内容的社交媒体成为品牌传播的主流通道，用户从单纯的接受广告信息转向参与品牌的共建，对品牌的信任建立在用户群的口碑和反馈上。用户参与的产品迭代循环机制以信息交流的方式在互联网上进行，能根据用户反馈不断升级换代的产品才会获得品牌竞争力。数字化时期的品牌策略也愈来愈注重产品衍生的情感价值和社会价值取向（图1）。与此同时，信息技术对旧有体制的冲击与新旧体制的交错，使问题的解决途径变得更为复杂，产生大量的抗解问题，比如信息爆炸带来的认知负荷超载和信息焦虑，物质丰富带来的过度消费、过度开发和环境问题，新的金融体系导致日趋严重的社会财富分配不均，全球化导致的地缘政治冲突和全球性的疫情蔓延，都是典型的"抗解问题"，都需要新的经验、综合性的解决方案和多个系统间的协调来解决（图2）。这些所谓的"抗解问题"使数字化时代的品牌概念超越了经济的范畴，涉及到个人、组织、机构和国家在复杂共生系统中对自身的定位和决策，而各人和组织处理信息的能力也成为维系自身发展的关键，主宰着未来的发展状态和生存体验。

在《系统思维》一书中，贾姆希德·加拉杰达吉[1]图示了人类智能的三个维度（图4），也揭示了科学、设计和艺术之间的互动关系。他认为科学是在差异性中寻找共性，艺术是在共性中寻找个性差异，而设计则是从许多不相关的单独元件中寻找构成新的整体的可行性。艺术实践在思维方法上求异，注重直觉，专注于对美和有意味的形式的探索和对人类情感的表达。同时，艺术构思的过程是使抽象观念成形的过程。在信息时代，艺术思维能提高对数字内容的表达能力和感染力，让内容更有创意，表达形式更加多元，避免内容和形式的同质化，能创造

1　Jamshid Gharajedaghi. *Systems Thinking: Managing Chaos and Complexity: A Platform for Designing Business Architecture*. New York: Kaufmann; 3rd Edition, 2011.

商品经济
ECONOMIC GOODS

80s 关注产品的物理质量
GOODS CENTERED

1980

图3 20世纪80年代后品牌发展的几个阶段

用户体验
USER EXPERIENCE

90s 关注用户需求和心理体验
USER VALUE CENTERED

1990

情感品牌
EMOTIONAL BRAND

00s 关注个人情感诉求和社会价值取向
SOCIAL VALUE CENTERED

2000

转型社会
TRANSFORMATION SOCIETY

10s 关注可持续未来和多元化价值观
ENVIRONMENT & CULTURE CENTERED

2010

AI与虚拟世界
MIXED REALITY & METAVERSE

20s 关注平行世界，建立AI时代的伦理价值观
REALITY & VIRTUAL REALITY CENTERED

2020

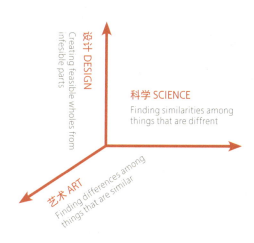

设计 DESIGN
Creating feasible wholes from infesible parts

科学 SCIENCE
Finding similarities among things that are diffrent

艺术 ART
Finding differences among things that are similar

图4 人类智能的三个维度 贾姆希德·加拉杰达吉

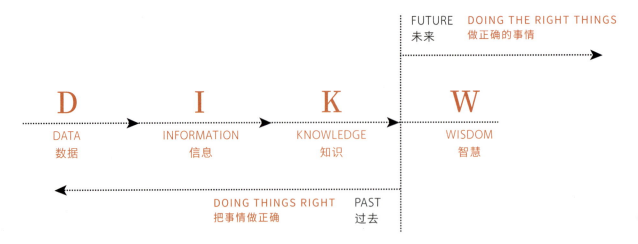

FUTURE   DOING THE RIGHT THINGS
未来   做正确的事情

D   I   K   W

DATA   INFORMATION   KNOWLEDGE   WISDOM
数据   信息   知识   智慧

DOING THINGS RIGHT   PAST
把事情做正确   过去

图5 改编自DIKW模型 Russell L. Ackoff, "From Data to Wisdom," Journal of Applied Systems Analysis 16 (1989): 39.

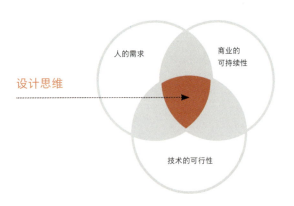

人的需求   商业的可持续性

设计思维

技术的可行性

图6 设计思维的定义

文化价值和多样化的社会文化生态，提升了生命体验。科学探索技术实现的可能性，将在信息时代提供更有效的物理和虚拟交互手段、更广泛的网络、更高的算力、更智能化的信息分析处理和更快捷的信息传递回馈。而如何在技术实现与成本之间协调，将实验室中的科学成果推广到全社会，则需要设计思维来规划和统筹。简单而言，设计思维是分析和取舍过程中发散性思维和聚敛性思维的有机组合，是决策中对信息进行综合比较和权衡，提出解决问题思路的思维方式。如同在DIWK模型（图5）中表述的一样，人类的知识建立在过去成功的经验上，数据被归纳为有条理的信息，信息被运用于实践，通过检验来获取知识。而智慧建立在过去的知识之上，针对未来的问题，创造性地提出问题方案，对未来作出正确明智的决策。设计思维也是创新的思维，正如IDEO的董事长蒂姆·布朗所说："设计思维是一种以人为本的创新方法，灵感来自设计师的方法和工具，它整合人的需求、技术的可能性以及实现商业成功所需的条件。"（图6）

今天，谷歌的在线字库可供选择字体有1400多种，蒙纳公司的MyFonts更是收集有13万以上的可选字体。曾经有人问美国字体设计师马修·卡特[2]："字库中已有这么多字体可供选择，为什么还要设计字体？"卡特回答说："因为每一个人都需要展示他们自己独特的声

2   Matthew Carter (1937年—)，出生于英国伦敦的世界级字体设计师，Georgia、Tahoma、Verdana、Meiryo字体都是他的作品，曾获2010麦克阿瑟奖。

音！"的确，独特的声音就是品牌要追求的。我想它至少包括两方面的考量。一是在商业环境中，面对同类商品的竞争，产品如何从同质化中突围；二是在数字化生存的环境里，品牌的物理特征被弱化，品牌要填充的是用户的需求和用户实现目标之间的空间。而每一个问题的解决方案都是一个变量，有不同的用户，就有不同的场景和情境，需要个性化的解决方案。大数据可以捕捉用户行为，并根据用户的生活模式和痛点来生成个性化解决方案，但它的基础是先认识到用户的价值和个体的独特性，从产品使用者的角度去思考问题。

2001年，马克·葛伯发表了《情感化品牌》[3]，提出了品牌策略的新策略，将关注点从产品转移到人，在品牌界掀起了一场革命。《情感化品牌》针对的是网络时代新的传媒方式，网络成为人们分享信息和交流信息的新媒介，人成为品牌创建战略中最关键的因素。《情感化品牌》强调产品的文化理念和用户内心愿景的契合，强调用户的个人身份（personal identity）、用户在现实中的挫折感（痛点）以及如何激发用户精神上超越现实的内心需求。给客户带来良好感觉的品牌，是可以改善他们的生活的产品，并且与他们的需求和愿望建立情感联系。品牌忠诚度是建立在信任的基础和价值观的认同上的。马克·葛伯的"情感品牌十诫"为产品开发提供了新的思路：比如产品要符合用户的生活方式；不要把用户当作消费者来看待，而是要作为值得尊重的人；产品不仅要满足物理需求，还必须满足客户的精神愿望。

数字化时代的产品不仅仅需要实现产品的使用价值。体验设计（UX Design）的缔造者唐·诺曼说："良好的以人为本的设计不仅仅是制作简单易用的有效工具；它与制作有效的工具来更好地融入我们的情绪相关，帮助我们表达我们的身份并支持我们的社交生活。"如（图3）中所示，随着数字化转型，产品策略的重心从使用价值延伸到个人价值和社会价值。在马斯洛的需求层级中（图7），当维持个体生存的缺失性基本需求得到保障后，成长性需求会随之升高。数字化时代的物质生活已经极为丰富，人们的需求更加注重群体感的归属、情感的联系和对内在价值的肯定。产品的象征意义、产品承载的文化内涵和价值取向成为产品需要传达的精神功能。2003年，唐·诺曼发表了《情感化设计》，提出了

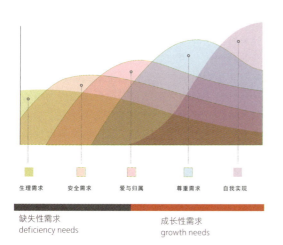

图7 [美]亚伯拉罕·马斯洛，《人类动机理论》（1943）

3   Marc Gobé, *Emotional Branding: The New Paradigm for Connecting Brands to People*, Simon & Schuster, 2001.

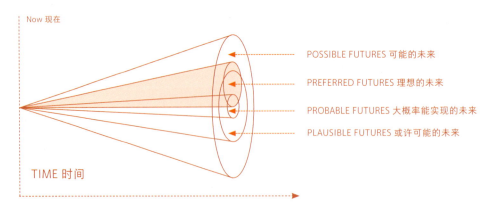

Now 现在

POSSIBLE FUTURES 可能的未来

PREFERRED FUTURES 理想的未来

PROBABLE FUTURES 大概率能实现的未来

PLAUSIBLE FUTURES 或许可能的未来

TIME 时间

图8　改编自未来之锥 （Source: Clement Bezold and Trevor Hancock，*An Overview of the Health Futures Field*，WHO Consultation, 1993）

情感设计的三个层次的理论：本能层次（Visceral），行为层次（Behavioral）和反思层次（Reflective）。本能层次是用户对产品的第一印象和直观的感觉。行为层次是用户在使用时对产品的功能性、易用性的关注，是产品的使用效果和整体的表现。而反思层次是产品与用户在文化取向和生活方式上意义的一致，是用户认同产品品牌的价值取向，认为品牌是用户自我形象的映射，代表了他们的社会身份。

《语义学转向：新的设计基础》[4]是另一本代表品牌理念转型的重要出版物。作者用符号学的框架来构建数字产品的"意义"。转型时期，数字产品全新的交互方式与用户的认知负载形成突出的矛盾，为改善数字化生存的产品体验，品牌的策略开始注重数字产品的易用性以及用户源于物理世界的心智模型。用户如何理解界面的心理认知模式、如何与产品的操作界面互动、如何轻松愉快地使用程序来完成自己的工作，成为数字情境中要考虑的新的"人的因素"。在1997年苹果全球开发者大会上，乔布斯说："你不能从技术开始，然后试着弄清楚它的卖点在哪里……对品牌策划来说最困难的事情是你如何建立一个有凝聚力的更大的愿景……你必须从客户体验开始，然后回溯到技术上……我们为苹果制定的战略和愿景，首先是我们可以为客户带来哪些令人难以置信的好处。"同样，亚马逊的品牌策略也是提倡"逆向

工作"，从产品或服务将为客户提供的核心价值开始，然后围绕客户没有得到满足的需求进行头脑风暴。他们让数字化生活更简单，让用户参与品牌共建，简化数字购物流程。比如他们率先推出的客户评论、一键式个性化推荐、Just Walk Out 无人收银购物车和气候承诺，使亚马逊在2021年名列全球市值第五。

抗解问题与未来思维

抗解问题一词是在20世纪60年代中期由霍斯特·里特尔[5]创造的，用来代表多维且极其复杂的问题。里特尔强调用设计思维的协同力量来为抗解问题提供解决方案。抗解问题互相纠缠，不断变化，在解决一个问题的同时又会衍生出更多的问题，很难有一个明确的解决途径。因此，抗解问题在提出之初就是以设计思维作为核心，这些复杂多维的问题需要一种协作方法来深入了解人类的根本需求、动机和行为。抗解问题为信息时代的品牌策略带来新的思路，使品牌的概念扩展到经济领域之外，在政治、文化、生态和伦理层面发挥越来越多的作用。品牌管理更是涉及到数字网络生态中的个人、团体、政府、国家的形象定位，而数据搜取、存储、传播、分析、处理的过程也跨越了技术层面，牵涉到政治、立法和伦理，直接影响了我们的思维方式和生活方式。

4　Klaus Krippendorff, *The Semantic Turn: a New Foundation for Design*, CRC Press, 2006.

5　Horst Rittel(1930–1990)，德国设计理论家。

20世纪70年代，维克多·帕帕奈克的书《为真实的世界设计》[6]一经发表，马上引发了设计界对设计的社会功能和社会批判功能的热议。书被翻译成25种语言，书中关于设计师的社会责任感和关注生态发展的思想被广泛传播。帕帕奈克认为"一项设计为实践其目的所经由的行为方式就是它的功能"。他将设计实践作为社会环境与生态环境中的一环来考量，呼吁诚实而适用的设计方式，不制造花哨的功能来诱惑和刺激商业销售。设计师要运用生态保护的框架来规划产品制作，设计方案需要对整体的生态负责，不助长浪费的风气。帕帕奈克的思想也代表了产品的社会功能，不仅是产品设计、生产过程中各个环节的协调，合理的产业结构和战略布局也包括对用户的行为方式进行反思与批判。

如何在信息社会为未来布局，设计方法如何为未来社会的战略规划提供思维的角度和建设性的方案？1994年，贝佐德和汉考克[7]用未来之锥图示了他们对未来可替代性方案的思考框架。（图7）图中呈现了未来在不确定性因素下的几种关系模式以及积极为未来做准备的意义。他们提议用基于事实、可测量和可观察的方法来建立未来场景，使未来战略的决策产生有远见卓识的创新规划，探索整体、综合和可替代的未来社会形态。这种为未来思考的系统方法将促进差异方之间的对话，让利益共享的各方参与并产生新知识和新经验，获得更深入的洞察力和具有普遍性的共识，这些都构成了猜测设计的核心。

2010年代，在社会转型期，思辨设计的反思更是全方位的，从社会公正、民权、气候变迁、生态环境、公共卫生到消费观念的反思，深入我们日常生活的各个方面。思辨设计对社会中习以为常的既成事实提出反思，旨在用新的观念来影响人们的想法和行为，用设计来激发人们的思考，影响人们未来决策和后续行动的改变，以此来创造一个更好的未来。思辨设计的代表人物安东尼·邓恩和菲奥娜·雷比提到："批判性设计使用猜测性的设计方案来挑战关于产品在日常生活中所扮演之角色的狭隘假设、成见和既定事实。[8] 它更多的是一种态度、一种立场而不是一种方法论。它的反面是肯定的设计：强化现状的设计。"安东尼·邓恩和菲奥娜·雷比期望将设计视为一种思辨的方式。"这种设计的形式依靠想象力，并致力于打开对抗解问题的新视角，从而对人类存在方式的诸多可能性进行进一步的讨论和争辩，激发和鼓励人们去自由想象。思辨设计可作为我们重新定义人和现实之间关系的催化剂。"在这里，思辨设计作为未来多样性（alternative futures）的催化剂，产品的概念是一种有可行性未来社会架构，这种预想的设计方案由跨学科领域的专业人员共同参与探讨，以思考者和参与者的态度，避开只关注短期目标的商业逐利主义，构想符合长远利益、更加多元、有更多选择性的未来生活场景和模式。

2020年被称为元宇宙元年，虽然实现其全部可能性所需的技术仍未完善，甚至很多人认为它只是一种商业炒作。然而，信息技术无疑又进入了一个新的阶段，以密码学为底层逻辑的区块链技术代表的去中心化、公开透明、不可篡改与匿名性将提供新的共识机制，进一步改变信息集成、需求分配以及信息网络的构建，提供更智能和有安全性能的模式。虚拟货币、NFT收藏品、游戏和虚拟世界中的电子商务和虚拟化身正成为品牌新的营销策略。随着虚拟技术的发展，元宇宙正提供这样一种设计预想，我们正站在一个与物理世界平行的虚拟新世界的门口，它的未来发展如何将取决于我们今天采取的行动，取决于我们为新世界搭建的地基与框架。

在访谈的章节，我们邀请了三位业界的专家从不同的角度来聊聊他们各自在信息设计领域的经验和观点。胡安·埃斯卡兰特来自著名的理工背景的跨界设计专业，长期从事交叉学科、生成设计、虚拟与现实的互动实践。约翰·德鲁长期致力于社区文化的打造，专注于无障碍设计与设计创新。庄稼昀长期在欧洲、北美从事独立戏剧和实验剧场。作为导演与剧构，她对写作与文本叙事观念、新的美学形式、故事叙述（storytelling）和故事生存（storyliving）都有独到的见解。希望三位专家的观点能给我们带来新的启发。

6　Victor Papanek, *Design for the Real World: Human Ecology and Social Change*, Pantheon Books, 1971.

7　Futures cone (Source: Clement Bezold and Trevor Hancock, *An Overview of the Health Futures Field*, WHO Consultation, 1993).

8　Anthony Dunne and Fiona Raby, *Speculative Everything Design, Fiction, and Social Dreaming*, The MIT Press, 2013.

扩散性思维和聚合型思维是设计思维的有机组成部分

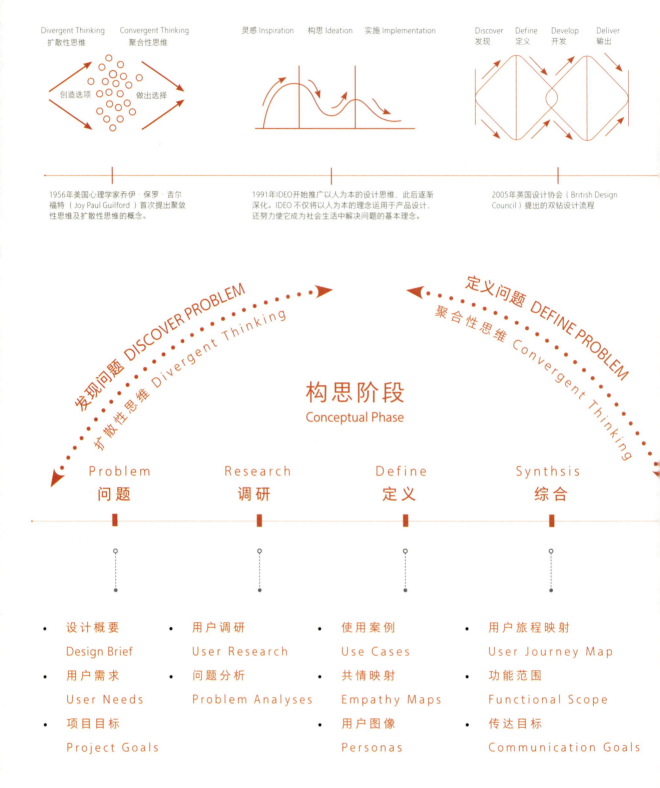

Divergent Thinking
扩散性思维

Convergent Thinking
聚合性思维

创造选项　　做出选择

灵感 Inspiration　　构思 Ideation　　实施 Implementation

Discover
发现

Define
定义

Develop
开发

Deliver
输出

1956年美国心理学家乔伊·保罗·吉尔福特（Joy Paul Guilford）首次提出聚敛性思维及扩散性思维的概念。

1991年IDEO开始推广以人为本的设计思维，此后逐渐深化。IDEO 不仅将以人为本的理念运用于产品设计，还努力使它成为社会生活中解决问题的基本理念。

2005年英国设计协会（British Design Council）提出的双钻设计流程

发现问题 DISCOVER PROBLEM
扩散性思维 Divergent Thinking

定义问题 DEFINE PROBLEM
聚合性思维 Convergent Thinking

构思阶段
Conceptual Phase

Problem
问题

Research
调研

Define
定义

Synthsis
综合

- 设计概要
  Design Brief
- 用户需求
  User Needs
- 项目目标
  Project Goals

- 用户调研
  User Research
- 问题分析
  Problem Analyses

- 使用案例
  Use Cases
- 共情映射
  Empathy Maps
- 用户图像
  Personas

- 用户旅程映射
  User Journey Map
- 功能范围
  Functional Scope
- 传达目标
  Communication Goals

用户是原点, 反馈与迭代机制是可持续发展的关键

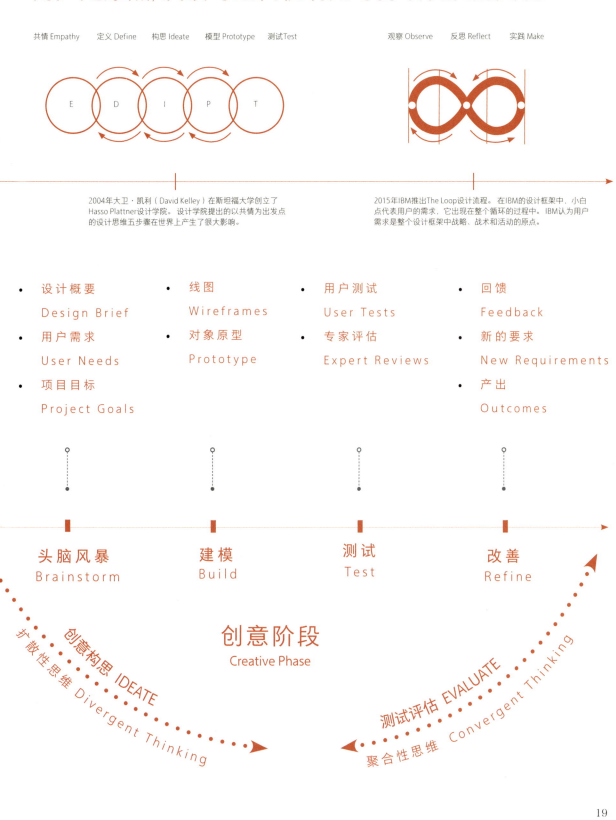

共情 Empathy　　定义 Define　　构思 Ideate　　模型 Prototype　　测试 Test

观察 Observe　　反思 Reflect　　实践 Make

2004年大卫·凯利（David Kelley）在斯坦福大学创立了Hasso Plattner设计学院。设计学院提出的以共情为出发点的设计思维五步骤在世界上产生了很大影响。

2015年IBM推出The Loop设计流程。在IBM的设计框架中，小白点代表用户的需求，它出现在整个循环的过程中。IBM认为用户需求是整个设计框架中战略、战术和活动的原点。

- 设计概要
  Design Brief
- 用户需求
  User Needs
- 项目目标
  Project Goals

- 线图
  Wireframes
- 对象原型
  Prototype

- 用户测试
  User Tests
- 专家评估
  Expert Reviews

- 回馈
  Feedback
- 新的要求
  New Requirements
- 产出
  Outcomes

头脑风暴
Brainstorm

建模
Build

测试
Test

改善
Refine

创意阶段
Creative Phase

创意构思 IDEATE
扩散性思维 Divergent Thinking

测试评估 EVALUATE
聚合性思维 Convergent Thinking

A / 02
品牌的内涵与发展

闵洁

一、品牌的内涵

我们正处在"品牌化"的时代,品牌随处可见地渗入人们的生活中。人们已经习惯以品牌的方式来解释世界的变化,热衷于追求时尚潮流和高品质的生活。事实上,"品牌"帮助人们在产品同质化的情况下区分产品、服务、消费价值等,他们不仅影响着我们的生活决定,而且改变了我们的生活方式。优秀的品牌在消费者心中占有不可替代的位置,这彰显着品牌无形资产的魔力。

正如美国营销大师米尔顿·科特勒所说:"在消费者与产品之间建立一种'爱'的忠诚度,需要一个传递情感的平台,这个平台就是品牌。"对品牌营销而言,成功的品牌往往超出物质层面,被赋予了丰富的情感因素,以精神价值联系受众的品牌将无往不胜。因此,品牌是企业内部每个人都认同与理解,是消费者、所有与之相关的人共有的体验与感受。时至今日,品牌已远非一个商标或销售工具,它为企业创造乐观积极的愿景,让消费者对品牌产生依恋,使生活走向人类共有经验中的精神层面和未来图景。

品牌的本质是沟通,它通过宣称产品所有权、提升品牌意识,展示了一种个性、价值观、态度以及社群归属身份的标记。尤其在今日的网络世界,内容生成者和内容传播者的角色已经融合在一起,品牌故事的讲述者与聆听者可以置换,品牌已经从单向传播迈入多向传播的时代。那么,品牌作为一种全方位的商业态度,企业需要在一个通用的价值观集合里,选择适合自己品牌的一种文化价值观加以演绎。可见,品牌需要解决的不仅是商业问题,更重要的是文化问题。例如,谷歌在创始之初,写下了著名的"我们信奉的十大真理"。研究核心工作后,谷歌明确普遍真理在其领域的重要性,这成为谷歌相信并尊崇的准则。由此,谷歌确立了它不仅是一个具有创新力的公司,更是一个为善的公司。

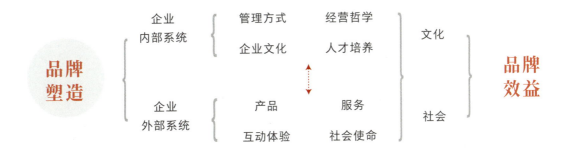

图1 品牌塑造的企业内外部系统

二、品牌塑造应对未来

人类的生命历程告诉我们，如果没有探索求知的意识，没有创新变革的设计，这个世界便没有价值。设计活动本身是一种复杂的人类行为，这些行为包括一系列的信息接收、认知、反馈等过程。作为品牌塑造的重要部分，它把"意义"赋予品牌，使其获得生命力。品牌战略的演变，是面对产业结构变化下的智慧价值的变化。品牌从体现优质产品或服务，变为企业与消费者、品牌的利益相关方、社会之间的关系枢纽，成为深层次的精神象征。因此，品牌塑造应对未来，需要在战略层面进行考量。首先，品牌塑造必须依靠独特而良好的品牌构建和形象设计，勾画出与众不同的品牌特性，令人印象深刻。其次，品牌塑造除了外在形象上的统一与规范，还需要建立品牌对于价值、质量、信誉的承诺与保障，作为人与世界互动的一种载体，品牌是发现与解决问题过程中的有效沟通。企业正是通过品牌的口碑或品质的力量快速成长，在消费者心目中形成强烈而持久的"品牌观念"。

如果品牌期望在海量的信息、纷繁的视觉环境中脱颖而出，必须认识到，互联网带来的便捷与低成本挑战同时也带来了新的契机。我们正从信息时代转向数字化时代，小而美的品牌可以借助网络渠道接触受众，小众化产品开始满足不同人群的需求，个性化需求被充分唤醒。品牌可以更全面地给予且改变消费者的感知、态度、行为，甚至信念。因此，企业要调整内外部系统来合力出击。企业的内部系统，包括管理方式、企业文化、经营哲学等；外在方式中，除了产品与服务，更要注重互动与体验、使命与社会责任等，以增强品牌有形与无形的效益。（图1）

显然，网络时代的品牌塑造需要掌握"如何说"，也就是，品牌语言的结构形式与传播方式起着关键性作用。人们处在虚拟空间与现实交融的情境里，品牌只有充分发挥想象才能获得认同与共鸣。这就需要品牌所传递的信息能引发消费者的好奇心并主动参与，同时运用智慧数据的"洞察力"进行多角度的媒体展示，以此挖掘群体共性，达到品牌传播效应。当品牌"真诚"发声、建立起与消费者的积极互动，就能赢得消费者的信任，从而为人们打开新视野。

A / 03
品牌塑造中的可视化设计

闵洁

一、 品牌塑造的信息整合

如果说数字化带给人类社会崭新的生存方式，信息设计则是这种生存方式的视觉化诠释。信息时代，人们无时不刻都在接受信息、处理信息、传播信息，而信息的存在方式也越来越多样化，并且显现出不同的层次。随着电子媒体双向性传播的发展与个人终端设备的普及，信息的接收和发送主体都发生了巨变，信息传播也随之而变。科技的飞速发展与信息渠道的四通八达，虽然给生活带来了便利，但也加快了工作和生活的节奏，人们变得更加忙碌与紧张，甚至出现了"信息过敏"以及信息发展所附带的混乱与压力下的"信息焦虑"。品牌塑造过程中，信息处理能力决定了信息的品质，而信息品质的差异会影响品牌传播的速度与强度。因此，品牌的策划与设计所传递的不仅是良好的感觉，还要增强品牌带来的归属感，这显示了文化精神在新环境中实现信息传达的优势。例如，小米公司创始以来，一直创造消费者的归属感，将"发烧友"圈层的友谊作为品牌的核心信息。

信息设计既是对信息的存储过程，也是对信息的加工与利用过程。自20世纪80年代信息设计学科确立以来，便形成了完整的信息设计理论与实践体系。信息设计是指以信息为起点，将信息视觉化视为信息传达目标的跨学科设计。信息设计作为一门前沿学科，不但涉及图形处理技术、信息技术，还涉及非技术领域的社会学、心理学、符号学等学科，其应用范畴日益宽泛，还扩大到了用户的交互体验、实时动态效果等新兴领域，对社会与经济的发展有着积极影响。在新媒体变革的背景下，信息设计的跨学科研究与实践趋势日益显著，信息设计也成为了应用于品牌塑造的一项重要课题。

品牌竞争环境早已今非昔比，几乎每个行业都陷入了"红海"之争。品牌策划是关系策略决策的重要因素。品牌策划的信息可视化设计是将品牌策划过程与策划内容的信息形式转换为视觉形式，以促进品牌的塑造与传播，这是品牌与信息设计共同发展的新方向。复杂的品牌信息数据可以通过组织、归纳和简化，将"品牌策划"整合到品牌核心竞争力的战略框架中，并进行直观而易读的视觉表达。信息设计的形象思维表达方式更贴近受众的认知识别与记忆规律，有利于品牌的信息整合，使品牌的内涵与策划方案达到有效的视觉呈现。此外，信息设计对于品牌塑造潜在的社会功能、激发社会创新等方面，都有着一定的推动作用。

二、 品牌的符号化表达

每个品牌的视觉形象都讲述着不同的品牌故事。意大利符号学家艾柯说："人是符号的动物，没有符号就没有人类社会。"认知心理学认为：在内部世界与外部世界之间存在着一种对应关系，人脑内部是以符号、符号结构以及符号操作来表征、解释外部世界的。品牌通过符号使人的内、外两个世界不断进行"信息交换"，从而加强人与外部世界的紧密连接，而这种连接越紧密，人的接受度也就越高。符号学是信息设计重要的理论依据，符号又是信息传达的媒介。首先，它可以在一定的文化语境下通过简明扼要的方式精准传达品牌内涵；其次，以创意性的符号设计突出品牌的象征性联想，拓宽品牌推广的边界；再次，通过各类符号的组合，品牌可以给予消费者一定的解码空间，留下鲜明的记忆。同时，随着符号的形态表达逐渐多元，特别是与新技术的结合，不仅使品牌的符号更加生动形象，而且给人以很强的心理暗示。

作为信息的视觉化符号，标志是人们认知品牌并与之沟通的一个载体。它必须具备能指和所指的双重特性，既是符号的形式，也具有符号的意义。古希腊语中，标识"logo"的拼写为"logoi"，意思是有影响力的宗教信仰或哲学观点。它是整个品牌视觉形象的灵魂，是企业的精神文化、信誉、服务特点的浓缩表现，是品牌个性要素的高度提炼。围绕标识所构成的品牌视觉形象，不仅加强了品牌竞争力，而且代表了品牌长期发展的精神符号。例如：耐克的勾形标志以古希腊神话中胜利女神的翅膀为原形，体现了自由与速度。耐克的所有努力传递着一致的信息：它代表青春与新锐，是很酷的品牌。但是，耐克并没有说"嗨，我们很酷"，而是说"just do it"（想做就做），广告语与标志形象相得益彰，激励人们购买耐克产品来体验运动生活，鼓励人们勇于面对各种挑战。标志所产生的积极意义不断影响着品牌的实践，并成为其品质的保证。

另一个典型案例就是苹果品牌，它铸就了这个时代的商业神话。事实上，苹果公司的成功在于出色地设计了产品的价值链。苹果公司打造出纵向整合型商业模式，使其在新技术产品赢得支持方面拥有明显优势。这种优势让苹果手机iPhone与运营商建立起一种不寻常的供求关系，从而掌握了渠道与品牌两个利器。从苹果品牌的价值来看，其卓越设计开创了软件操作人性化的先河，吸引了全球的粉丝和用户。被咬掉一口的"苹果"标志拓展了观者的视觉乐趣，苹果公司尝试一系列的视觉形式，从五彩条的苹果标志，到2013年变更并沿用至今的扁平化风格的纯色logo，持续加深了人们对"苹果"引领时代潮流的印象。而"苹果"作为符号的涵义覆盖了西方社会的三大方面：科技、人文、宗教。科技的苹果，是牛顿在苹果树下思考而发现了万有引力定律，寓意着苹果品牌致力于科技创新；人文的苹果，在希腊神话中象征着最美女神，这场金苹果之争，导致了历时10年的特洛伊战争，这预示了品牌对美的不懈追求；宗教的苹果，是圣经故事中伊甸园里的智慧之果，它无疑成了智慧的代名词。"苹果"这三方面交错重叠的信息释放出符号的多重意义，满足了消费者的想象，使品牌拥有了无限的生命力。21世纪突破性品牌的发展趋势、商业模式与平台化的创新使品牌的延伸度不断扩大，这为品牌形象传播提供了很大的创意空间。

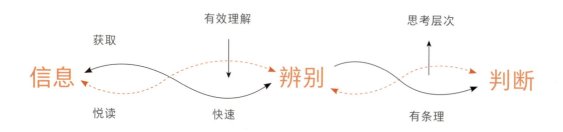

有效理解

获取

思考层次

信息 ⇄ **辨别** → **判断**

悦读　　　　快速　　　　　　　有条理

图1 品牌策划信息可视化的互动机制

三、品牌策划可视化的本义

当今，我们正处于一个"信息超载"和"信息污染"并存的时代。当五花八门的信息扑面而来时，人们对触手可及的信息无所适从。所以，那些富有想象力、直观明了的视觉信息图，特别是通过深入分析，集图像、符号、数字、文字解读于一体的信息设计图解，不禁让人流连忘返。美国图表信息设计家乌尔曼说："我们正在将信息技术与信息建筑予以嫁接，成功的视觉信息设计是被铸造的成功建筑、被凝固的音乐，信息理解是一种能量。"与此同时，品牌逐渐将数据应用于营销实践，主要是以消费者随时随地的个性化、碎片化需求为中心，使消费者的沟通变得更为即时而有效。

交互信息改变了传统的传播模式，每个人都可能成为信息传播的中心点。品牌策划可视化的本义，是经过对品牌的分解、整理、策划，进行秩序化设计的创作行为，从理性到感性、从时间到空间、从分解到融合，这是一个不断求索的逻辑思维的过程。信息设计在展示品牌核心概念的基础上，运用视觉传达设计手法，解析各种构成要素和组成部分，通过创意与策划向受众传达品牌价值观。品牌策划方案不再需要厚厚的文字稿来陈述，而是以确凿的信息数据和具有表现力的图像符号将复杂问题清晰化，生动有趣地揭示出内在的联系，这是一种卓有成效的沟通方式与传播途径。其可视化的沟通方式是信息获取与信息悦读双向并驱的过程（图1），旨在实现如下目标：

· 提供单纯文字无法给予的阅读乐趣
· 帮助人们快速而有效地理解信息内容
· 引导人们进入有条理的思考层次
· 凸显品牌策划特色、让人记忆深刻

品牌策划可视化设计在新媒介的情境中拓展品牌策划的商业和社会运用空间，并从中达到认识上的超越，力图展现策划方案的逻辑思维方式。运用图片、视频、动画、信息图表等可视化设计逻辑性强、内容丰富的优势，也成为了品牌在社交媒体上必不可少的推广利器。因此，设计者要学会组织逻辑语言和多样性媒介表达方法，还要擅长将策略思考与信息剖析能力相结合，这样才能帮助人们对品牌信息进行正确的重构、认知、记忆和取用。它的发展前景趋于成为连接认知心理学和人工智能研究之间的桥梁，这将引领我们走进无比奇妙的领地。

A / 04
品牌策划信息可视化构筑

闵洁

信息设计中，原始信息要经过一系列的加工与提炼，才能将数据信息转化为视觉信息、文字语言转化为视觉语言、抽象概念转化为具体形象。数据可视化设计侧重于展现数据的事实，而品牌策划可视化设计则侧重于解析与传达信息。品牌策划的可视化图解，首先，需要依据统计学原理，对原始数据信息进行收集、整理、分析和归纳；其次，通过逻辑思维方式来梳理信息的关系与结构；再次，信息沟通形式必须符合认知习惯和心理活动规律；最后，根据符号学原理对整体视觉表达进行创意与设计。其步骤主要包括：一、调研与信息收集；二、品牌概念确定；三、信息要素提炼；四、视觉逻辑结构建立；五、信息视觉转化。（图2）

一、调研与信息收集

在进入设计之前，要开展调研与信息收集的工作。主要是对策划案的决定性因素，如定位、目标、内容、模块等进行分析与判断，同时确定信息的维度与层次关系。虽然市场调研已经变为搜集与解释数据的商业学科，但是品牌策划中的洞察力也是必不可少的，它来自对人性、文化、社会等方面更为深入的观察方法。

对于品牌而言，市场调研是收集、评估和影响受众对产品、服务和品牌偏好的数据。其中，对潜在消费者的态度、意识和行为的新见解往往决定了品牌未来发展的机会，可用信息将成为更为主要的决策依据。数据本身并不能提供答案，分析与解释数据是一种研究技能。信息设计者可以邀请调研公司协助完成调研，或者自行组织调研与搜集。需要注意的是，信息收集要始终围绕目标和主题设定展开，避免淹没在浩瀚的信息海洋中找不到方向。

二、品牌概念确定

品牌策划可以说是基于品牌理念或价值，在特定环境下所展开的想法、愿景或计划，经过创造性的迭代过程，形成具体的解决方案。品牌策划的首要任务是挖掘出目标客户对某个产品或品牌复杂信息背后的隐藏动机，当揭示出潜在的价值观和信念时，就能保证品牌要传达的信息是富有意义的。这里所说的品牌核心概念，是品牌明确现阶段的目标方向，需要基于企业的"使命"和"愿景"来进行规划。以星巴克为例，它将自身定

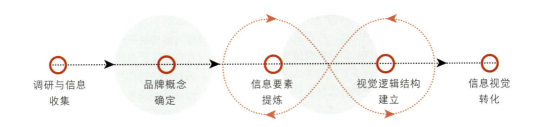

图2 品牌策划信息可视化设计步骤

调研与信息收集　品牌概念确定　信息要素提炼　视觉逻辑结构建立　信息视觉转化

位为人的事业而非咖啡生意，针对消费者的潜在需求，将核心概念确定为消费者提供"第三空间"，即除家庭和职场以外的第三个休闲场所。因此，品牌核心概念要连同考虑其他因素，达成创意与执行、成本和效能之间的平衡与和谐。

随着互联网+、大数据、数字营销、移动化等概念的不断升级，品牌策划面临着前所未有的多元化选择。这已经不再是营销策划者的时代，而是营销共舞者的时代。品牌策划的信息设计不再以单一的创意为主，而要求视其为一个系统工程。实现核心概念的问题，涉及品牌塑造与策划的关联度、相关品牌活动与主题的具体实施，甚至还要拓展商业创新等新视角。此时，需要根据品牌策划目标确定一个标题名称，简明扼要地概括信息图解的内容，生动而准确地表达目标内容。

三、信息要素提炼

在信息过剩的今天，品牌策划可视化的重点是对信息要素的提炼，也就是对可用信息进行有效的统筹与提取。信息设计要素是指构成信息结构系统必不可少的文字、图形、符号、色彩等视觉要素，它是信息的视觉载体，信息必须依靠这些载体才能实现传播。信息要素的提炼，通过基本形式设计和结构设计来确保视觉形式的独特性。首先，要根据策划目标来确定中心概念的信息。其次，对已收集的信息进行筛选，去芜存菁地保留高价值的信息。最后，核实所用信息的可信度来确保信息提取的质量。因此，构建起清晰、明确、合理的信息关系是信息设计要素提炼的关键所在。

整个信息要素提炼的过程要考虑品牌创新和品牌策划之间的共生原则。其一，必须确定品牌的调性来引发有创造力的视觉表现，这体现了品牌与受众之间的一种互动关系。其二，它是为解决问题而进行的创作，以提供用户价值为中心，比如以新视野、新市场、新目标群体和新产品概念等动态的方式，使信息设计要素有利于体现品牌策划的主旨。其三，在内容、形式方面能够凸显品牌与众不同的特征，充分展现品牌的活力。其四，它不仅仅限于营销传播，还为品牌开发者和利益相关者提供品牌策划方案的视觉解释和视觉引导。

四、视觉逻辑结构建立

视觉逻辑结构建立是品牌策划可视化图解的重要环节。信息逻辑结构是指时间、空间、数量、位置等信息维度之间的组织结构，它反映了信息单元之间的内在联系，是信息要素之间的层次、秩序关系的显现结构。此阶段与信息要素提炼有着重叠与往复的关系，一般会在纸上绘制草图，在绘制过程中还可以对信息要素查漏补缺，将版式分布大致确定下来。与此同时，还要协调品牌信息传达的主次关系，在以核心信息为根本的基础上附加次级信息，形成品牌策划可视化图解的一致性与连贯性。

视觉逻辑结构的建构以高质量的信息要素为基础，经过反复提炼与重组后，其结构可以用树状图、流程图、桥型图等形式，清晰地显示信息集群和信息单元之间的逻辑关系，从而起到视觉引导的作用。这对信息设计中的版面设计提出了更高的要求，尤其需要将信息进行层级区分的设计处理。从视觉逻辑上看，要在体现主题理念的同时，具有清晰可循的视觉轨迹，使受众更加条理化地获取信息，并且能够迅速觉察到信息之间的关系和本质意义，方便受众把握策划方案的主旨，加深对该品牌方案的印象。可见，信息版面的控制能力取决于设计者所兼具的良好策划能力和设计能力。

五、信息视觉转化

信息设计的目的在于创造与满足人们获取信息时得到的情感和审美享受。显然，有趣而富有感染力的品牌策划可视化图解，不但能够使观者一目了然、饶有兴趣，而且具有很强的说服力，它直观反映了品牌的战略性决策。信息视觉转化，是指将信息形式或者信息内容转换为观者易于解读的视觉化结果，有机地将信息结构与信息要素以视觉化形式组织起来。事实上，提高信息的审美价值来引发信息接受者的"视觉愉悦"是信息设计的重要手段。信息视觉转化的优劣决定了受众对品牌策划的认可度。因此，必须考虑信息接受者对品牌策划的认知过程中视觉和心理感知的相互作用。

此阶段的信息设计，一方面要协调好策划内容和品牌特性之间的关系，另一方面要在品牌的当前消费者或潜在消费者的价值观趋向上达成一致。宏观的信息视觉转化中，设计者应采用合理的布局来强化信息结构的阅读次序，帮助受众迅速理解内容进度、内容构架。微观的信息视觉转化，主要是指信息要素的视觉转化。信息要素包括文字、色彩、索引线、标注等的大小、空间的设计考量，同时还应考虑信息呈现的多种表现形态，如平面、立体、静态、动态、空间等类型。无论何种表现形式，信息视觉转化离不开发现问题、思考问题与解决问题的品牌策略性思考。

总而言之，有意义的品牌策划图解需要全方位展示符合受众心理需求的品牌策划方案。它能够抓住所要传递的信息内容的本质，具备层次清晰、结构严谨、造型独特、表达准确等特征。优秀的品牌策划图解往往围绕主题展开多样的互动传播，这为品牌的网络营销开拓了新空间，也使得信息设计发展具有更多的可能性。信息要素的动态延伸成为了品牌策划可视化的方向，它所构筑的互动意义为品牌传播提供了开放的舞台。而品牌策划项目的创意性是将体验、场景、感知、美学等消费者的主观认知，建立在文化传统、科技迭代、商业利益等企业生态上。信息设计在助力品牌策划的过程中，传递出营销传播的新理念与跨专业实践的新探索，成为了拓展品牌策划视觉叙述的新亮点。

B/
01

实验作品对话

日常生活数据可视化

DAILY LIFE DATA VISUALIZATION

指导教师
王琛 Chen Wang
闵洁 Min Jie

作品形式
数据可视化
Data Visualization

班级:
CSUF 483E
SIVA 品牌战略与管理班

上海视觉艺术学院和加州州立大学（佛卢顿）两校合作的一个设计教学项目。课程通过收集个人日常生活数据，指导学生用定量的方法对数据进行梳理和比较。通过对视觉可视化方法的学习，学生们尝试通过分析原始数据的内在关联性来寻找规律，学习从生活中观察和记录自己的行为，定义行为模式中的特性和步骤，运用设计思维从行为模式中分析生活中潜在问题的根源和关联性，寻找改善生活体验和提升自我的契机以及新的解决问题的思路。

A design project in cooperation between CSUF and SIVA. Through the collection of daily life data, the course guides students to use quantitative research methods to sort out and compare the data. Through the study of visual visualization methods, students find patterns by analyzing the internal correlation of raw data, define behavior patterns in life from observation and analysis, learn methods of defining problems from context, and look for opportunities to improve life experience and self-improvement, as well as new ways of solving problems.

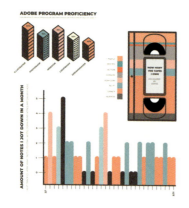

图1 数据可视化 Ana Lares

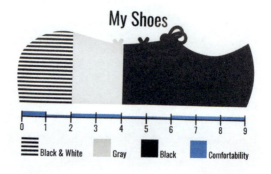

图2 数据可视化 Ashley Tam

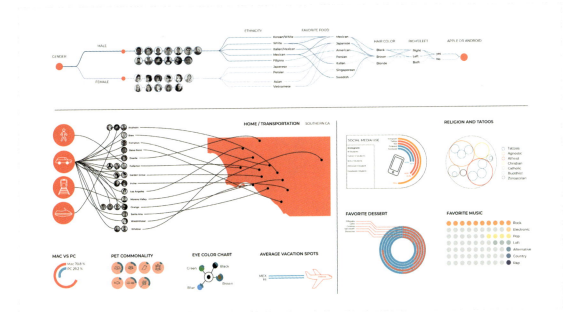

图3 数据可视化 Jared Spellman

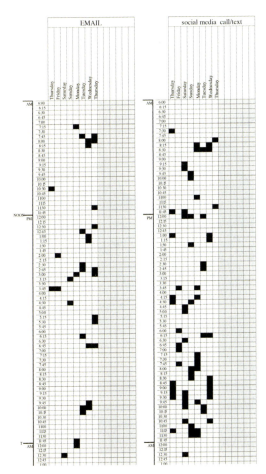

图4 数据可视化 Samuel Arellano

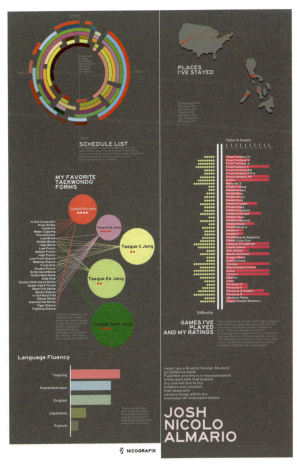

图5 数据可视化 Josh Nicolo Almario

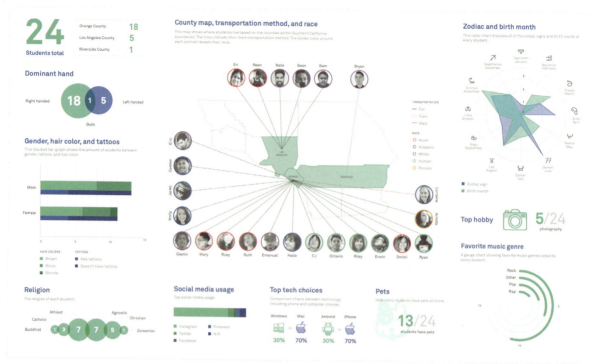

图6 数据可视化 Mary Tron

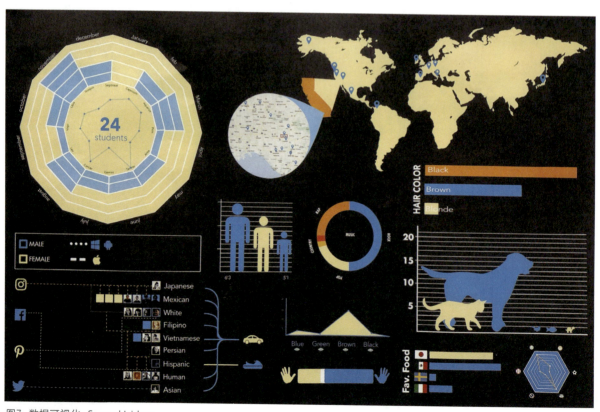

图7 数据可视化 Samuel Isidoro

32

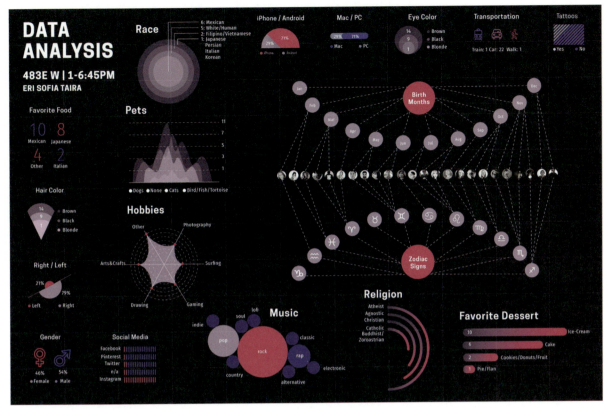

图8 数据可视化 Eri Spfia Taira

图9 数据可视化 Ashley Tam

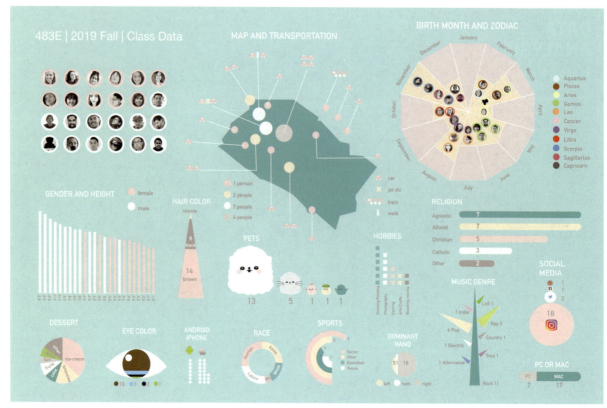

图10 数据可视化 Duong Rosy

图11 数据可视化 Damaris Paz

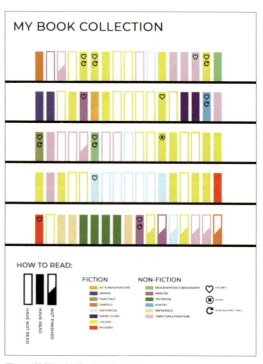

图12 数据可视化 Eric Rubalcava

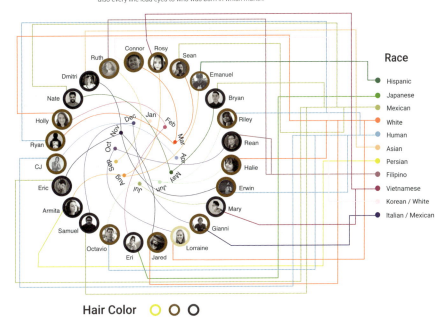

图13 数据可视化 Armita Bastani

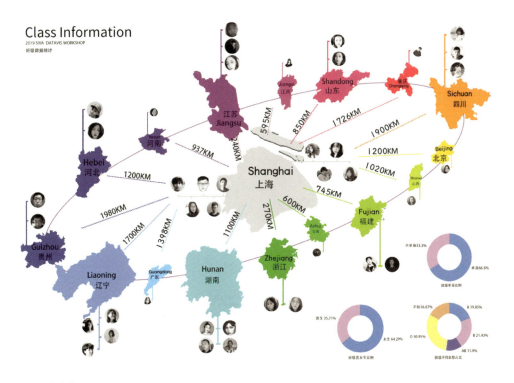

图14 数据可视化 孔嘉伟

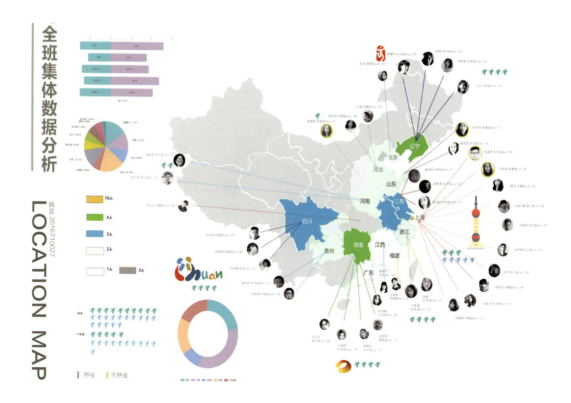

图15 数据可视化 韩芸

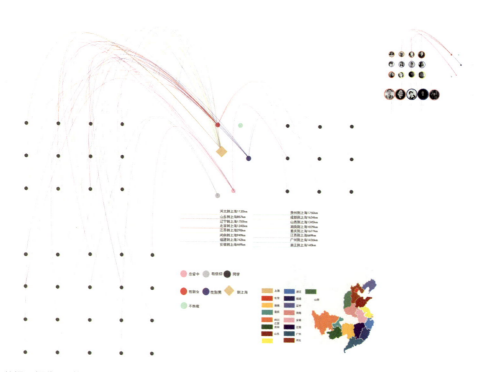

图16 数据可视化 王瀚瑶

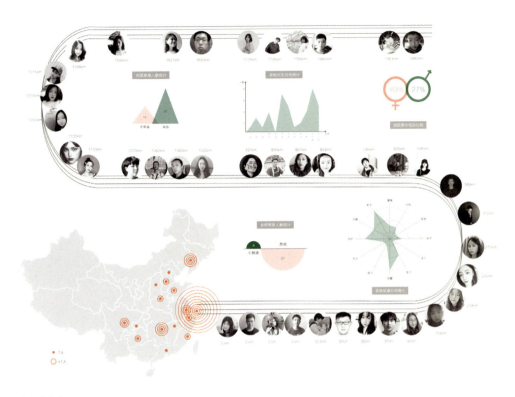

图17 数据可视化 叶宛维

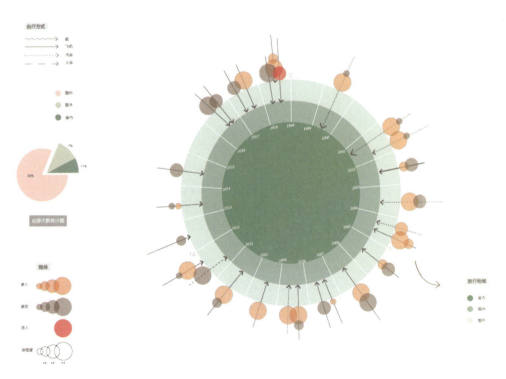

图18 数据可视化 叶宛维

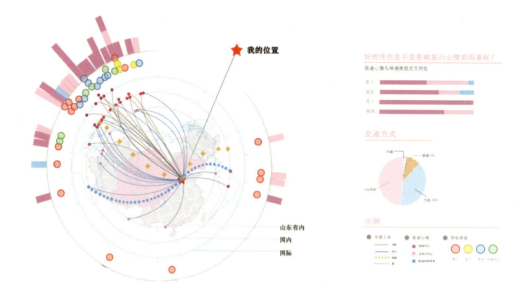

图19 数据可视化 曲咏雪

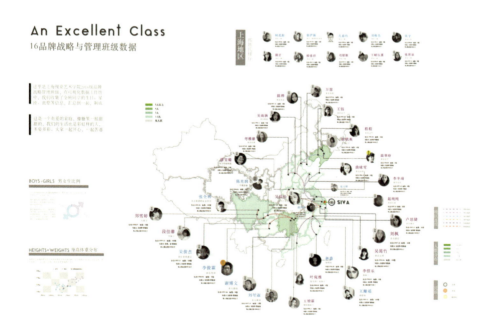

图20 数据可视化 曲咏雪

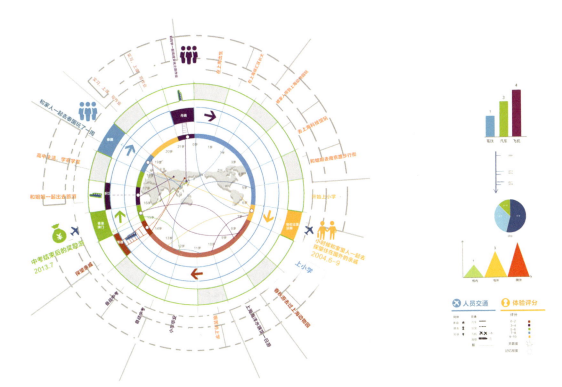

图21 数据可视化 曲咏雪

图22 数据可视化 金伊强

中介语艺术项目: 英语觉句
INTERLANGUAGE ART: ENGLISH JUEJU

作者姓名
乔纳森 · 思道林 Jonathan Stalling
王琛 Chen Wang

作品形式
中介语艺术
社会服务设计
Interlanguage Art
Social Service Design

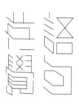

中介语是母语与第二语言之间的交错地带，中介语艺术试图从这个中间地带中寻找艺术表现的灵感，而英语绝句是乔纳森 · 思道林和王琛共同合作的一个关于诗歌和感知的中介语艺术项目。该项目由"Jue：绝"和"Jue：觉"两部分组成。第一部分在美国向西方民众介绍中国古典诗歌的音韵格律和天人合一的宇宙观，将诗歌作为一种语言工具来探索外在的自然与内在的心灵。"Jue：绝"运用英语、音韵和绝句的艺术形式来表达情感和认知。第二部分的"Jue：觉"试图打破语言和学科界限，利用数字技术、编程语言和算法，拓展人类知觉的感知领域并整合与感知相关的记忆、情感与认知，探索数字化的诗意表达和契合数字时代语境的新的认知感悟。

Interlanguage is the intersection of a first language and a second language. Interlanguage art seeks inspiration for artistic expression from this intermediate region, and English Jueju is a project of interlanguage art by Jonathan Stalling and Chen Wang. It consists of two parts, one is to introduce Chinese classical poetry and cosmology to Western audiences, use poetry as a language tool to experience nature and explore one's inner world, meanwhile, to teach Westerners to write English Jueju. The second part attempts to transcend language and disciplinary boundaries, expand the perceptual field of human cognition, and use digital technology, programming languages and algorithms to explore poetic expressions that fit the context of the digital age.

图1 乔纳森·思道林和王琛合著的书籍 YINGGELISHI, 香港大学美术博物馆出版,芝加哥大学出版社北美发行

图2 在书中,两位作者用对话的方式讨论了中介语艺术的理论和实践方法

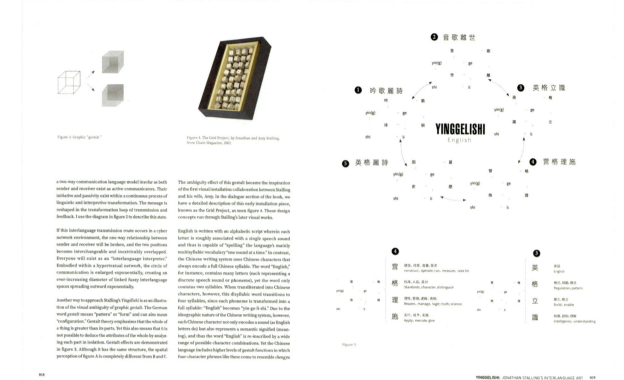

图3 王琛阐述了中介语艺术的理论和方法

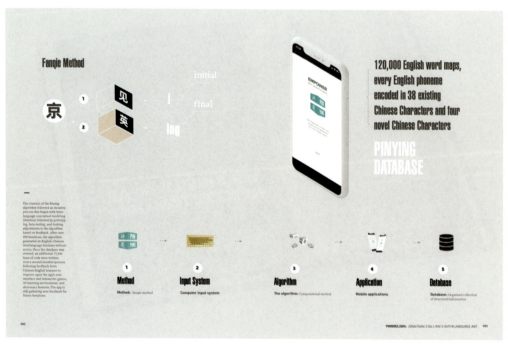

图4 乔纳森·思道林介绍了中介语艺术的实践

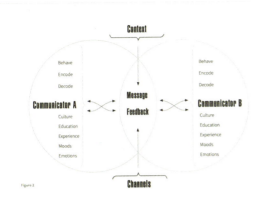

Figure 2

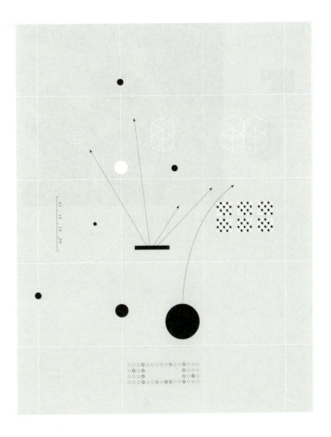

Jakobson's principle of equivalence contains important concepts: the equivalence principle, selection axis, and combination axis. This is the key to understanding the poetic function of language, including Stalling's interlanguage works like his Sinophonic English opera *Yíngēlìshí*. In this work, the receiver selects and superimposes the phonetic symbol code according to her own native language environment (in this case Chinese), and this filtering results in a completely different, context-specific process of semantic decoding. In this sense the protagonist of the opera decodes the English she is hearing and encodes the English she is speaking entirely within the phonology of her native language, Mandarin Chinese. In his introduction to the published libretto of *Yíngēlìshí*, Stalling describes his compositional method: "Just attend to the frequency of sound—the opening of Chinese vibrations beneath the surface of each English word. Words appear as Chinese syllables rearranged into English syntax and diction; as Chinese makes a home in English, it becomes English without having stopped being Chinese."

Stalling provides an example from the libretto: "please forgive me" becomes "pú lì sì, fó gěi fú mí 普利私，佛给浮谜,"

which he translates as "vast private profits, Buddha offers impermanent mysteries."

He describes each line of the opera as a "combination lock" that he "kept turning . . . around again and again," producing nearly "limitless choices for each line." "Eventually," he writes, "I would alight upon a set configuration of Chinese characters that began to create a poetically charged field of meaning and feeling (often this took place as a voice coming from behind the Chinese)."

Thus, Stalling's method distances itself from an intralingual act of communication insofar as the sender employs one set of language norms to communicate content to a receiver who uses another set of language norms to decode it. In actual practice, we see pronunciation acting as an interlanguage space enhancing rather than delimiting the uncertainty of linguistic meaning as words toggle between two language codes. What is more, his interlanguage work operates within

5. Jonathan Stalling, *Yíngēlìshí: Sinophonic English Poetry and Poetics* (Denver: Counterpath Press, 2011), 4–5.

图5 王琛介绍了中介语艺术的理论和方法

图6 王琛设计的书籍内页插图

图7 英语觉句团队在准备教学视屏的拍摄

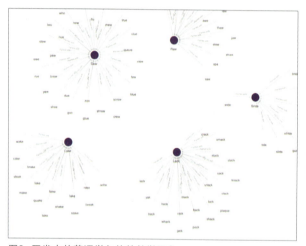

图8 开发中的英语觉句软件教学平台

图9 Jue的四个中文同音字代表了"觉句"探索的四个方面和最终目标

图10 英语觉句音韵教学模块

图11 英语觉句项目的图示

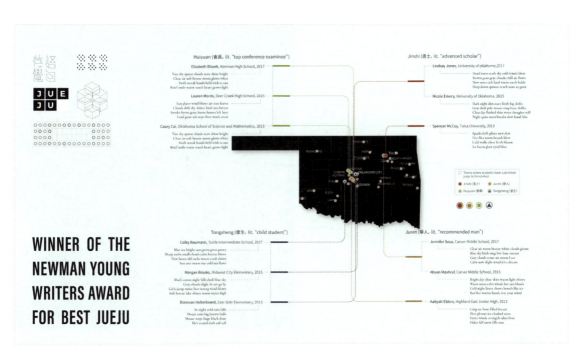

图12 乔纳森·思道林为推动英语绝句发展而设立的纽曼青年作者奖（Newman Young Writer Award）

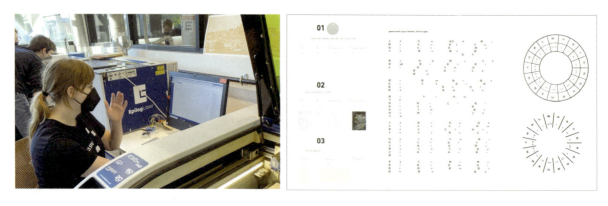

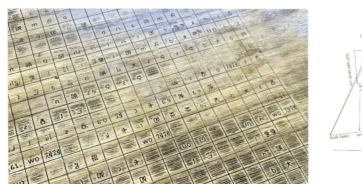

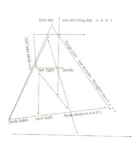

图12-16 英语觉句项目在美国堪萨斯城市艺术研究院（Kansas City Art Institute）举办的工作坊项目。项目与该院写作、视觉传达和版画三个专业的师生共同合作，版画图形由米格尔·里维拉（Miguel Rivera）教授制作提供，2021年

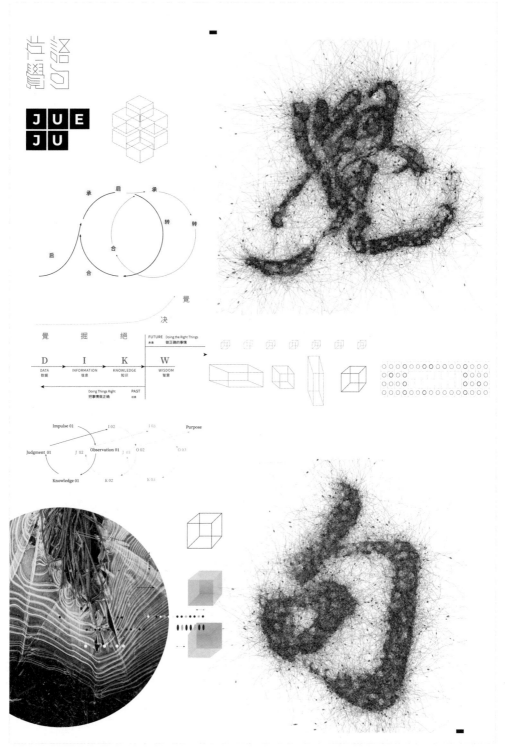

图17 英语觉句项目应邀在2022年中国可视化与可视分析大会艺术项目（China VISAP'22）上展示并作主题演讲

B/
02

—

文化类

互动设计课程标识与作业
DESIGN FOR INTERACTIVE ART

作者姓名
王琛 Chen Wang

作品形式
数码
Digital

班级:
CSUF 483F

483F是加州州立大学（佛卢顿）的互动设计课程。教学内容包括介绍东西方不同时期的编码方法，比如《易经》、二进制、摩尔斯编码和苏州码。二进制是计算机技术的基础，它只使用了 0 和 1 两个数字。目前，全球互联网上使用的网页和电子邮件一般使用二进制Unicode和美国ASCII标准码进行信息交换。包括苏州码在内的中文编码字符集GB18030也是Unicode的组成部分，这意味着苏州码不仅是承载中国传统文化的技术手段，也是现代电子技术和数字信息传播技术的组成部分，是介绍信息文化史时不可缺少的一页。

483F is an interactive design course at CSUF. When introducing the history of coding, I will cover different coding methods in the East and the West, such as binary and Suzhou numerals. Binary is the basis of computer technology, it only uses two numbers 0 and 1. Currently, web pages and e-mails used on the Internet generally use binary Unicode and American ASCII standard codes. The Chinese coded character set GB18030, including Suzhou numerals, is also a part of Unicode, which means that Suzhou code is not only a technical means to carry Chinese traditional culture, but also an indispensable part of digital information technology.

图1 作品展示场景

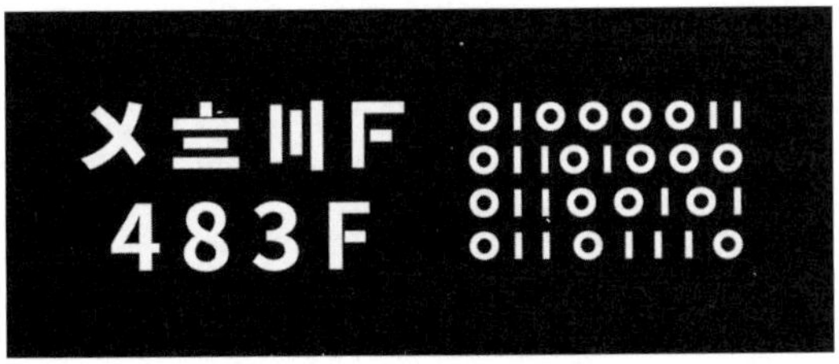

图2，3 将483F用不同的方法生成代码，比如用二进制的0和1字符，并按Binary的标准方式转换成代码，如4是00110100，8是00111000，3是00110011，F是01000110

Letter	ASCII Code	Binary
4	052	00110100
8	056	00111000
3	051	00110011
F	070	01000110

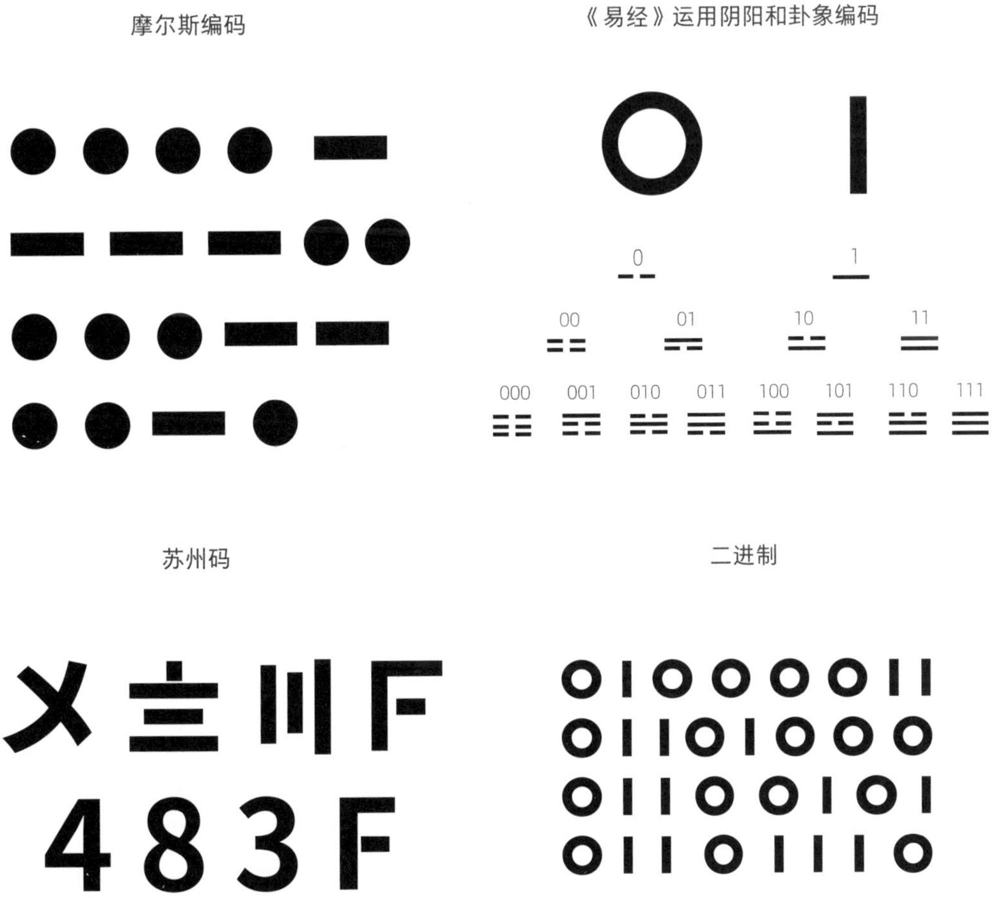

摩尔斯编码

《易经》运用阴阳和卦象编码

苏州码

二进制

图4-7 将483F用不同的方法生成代码

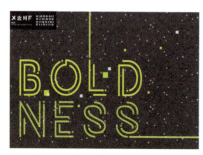

图8-13 学生作品 Michelle Jayme

图14，15 学生作品 Margaret Zisk　　图16，17 屏幕展示

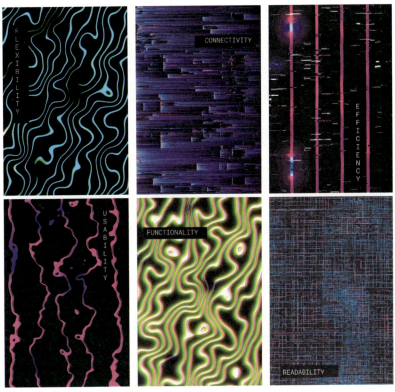

图18-23　学生作品　Fray Munoz

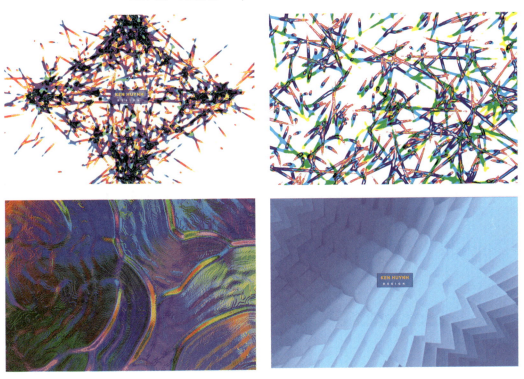

图24-27　学生作品　Ken Huynh

贝戈维奇画廊数字档案馆

IMPACT! BEGOVICH GALLERY 50 YEARS EXHIBITION DIGITAL ARCHIVE

作者姓名
王琛 Chen Wang
布莱恩·戈麦斯 Bryan Gomez

作品形式
品牌策划 视觉设计
Branding Planning / Visual Design

图1，2 贝戈维奇画廊内部，照片由贝戈维奇画廊提供

图3 数码展示台 Mary Tron

在过去的50年里，贝戈维奇画廊为文化多样性做出了贡献，并将社区凝聚在一起。画廊坚信艺术应该贯穿所有学科，它不仅限于创作和表达，而应该是每一个人都可以参与的对话。它是一个具有多样性和包容性的空间，可供来自社会不同背景的个人和群体共同参与和合作。在画廊成立50周年后，数字档案馆将继续以数字虚拟的方式让公众浏览过去展出的作品和艺术家以及艺术活动的相关信息，并利用新的互动理论和技术为民众带来新的互动体验，继续延续文化的影响力。

Over the past 50 years, Begovich Gallery has contributed to cultural diversity and brought communities together. The gallery firmly believes that art should permeate all disciplines. It is not limited to creation and expression, but should be a conversation that everyone can participate in. It is a diverse and inclusive space where individuals and groups from different backgrounds of society can participate and collaborate together. After the gallery's 50th anniversary, the digital archive will continue to allow the public to browse past works, artists and related information about art activities in a digital and virtual way, and use new interactive theories and technologies to bring new interactive experiences to the public, to continue the cultural influence.

图4-6　贝戈维奇画廊的出版物以及撤展作品，照片由贝戈维奇画廊提供

#FD855A　#EDE367　#F98282　#EEEAD4　#54ACEF

Key words:
community,
system,
circle,
engagement,
impact.

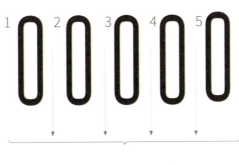

图7-9　"50年影响"标识的字体色彩和创意表达

图10 户外海报

图11 网页

图12，13 标识的推广运用

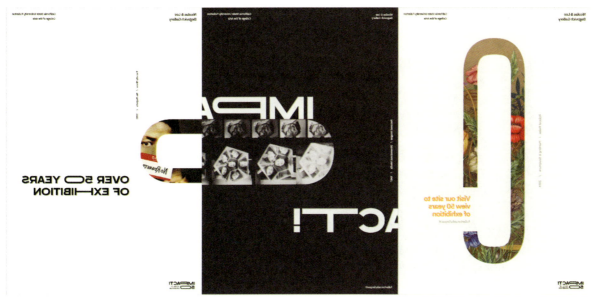

图14 网页

图15 网站导航系统

图16，17 网站页面

图18 海报

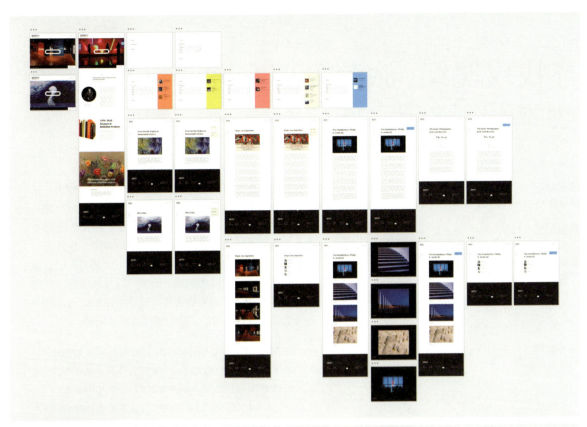

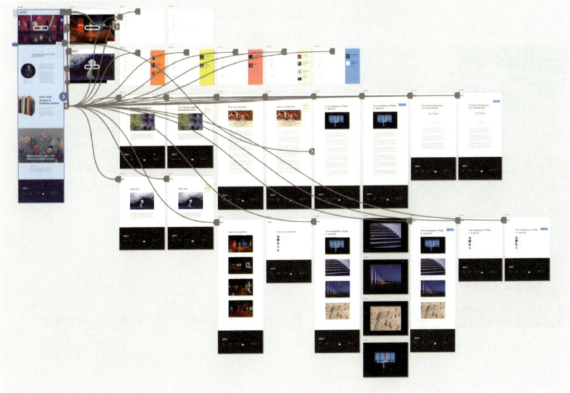

图19，20 网站信息架构

寻找玫瑰红：旅游策划方案
LOOKING FOR ROSE RED: TOURISM PLANNING PROJECT

作者姓名
陈颖超 Chen Yingchao

作品形式
品牌策划
信息设计
包装设计
Branding Planning
Information Design
Packaging Design

指导教师
闵洁 Min Jie

上海作为全国旅游热点城市，不仅是因为它的繁华，更是因为它岁月沉淀后的魅力。历史的沉积造就如今摩天大楼与花园洋房、弄堂街道并存的现象。而20世纪30年代大上海的名媛、明星代表人物，如张爱玲、阮玲玉、周璇等依旧被人们所迷恋。调研显示，文艺青年们普遍对这些文化有着浓厚的兴趣。开发"寻找玫瑰红"旅游线路，可以让老上海名媛文化与短途旅游相结合。其内容包括设计路线、推广活动和辅助主题活动等。

As a national tourist hotspot, Shanghai is attractive not only because of its prosperity, but also because of its charm after long years of precipitation. The historical deposition has created the phenomenon of skyscrapers coexisting with the garden houses, alleys and streets now. Celebrities and movie stars of Shanghai in the 1930s, such as Eileen Chang, Ruan Lingyu, Zhou Xuan, etc. are still fascinated by people. Surveys show that literary youth generally have a strong interest in this culture. As a result, the "Looking for Rose Red" tour route is developed, so that the culture of old Shanghai celebrities can be combined with short-distance tour. This project includes route design, promotional activities, and ancillary theme activities.

图1 "寻找玫瑰红"活动衍生品设计

娱乐旧址　　花园洋房　　弄堂　　历史名校

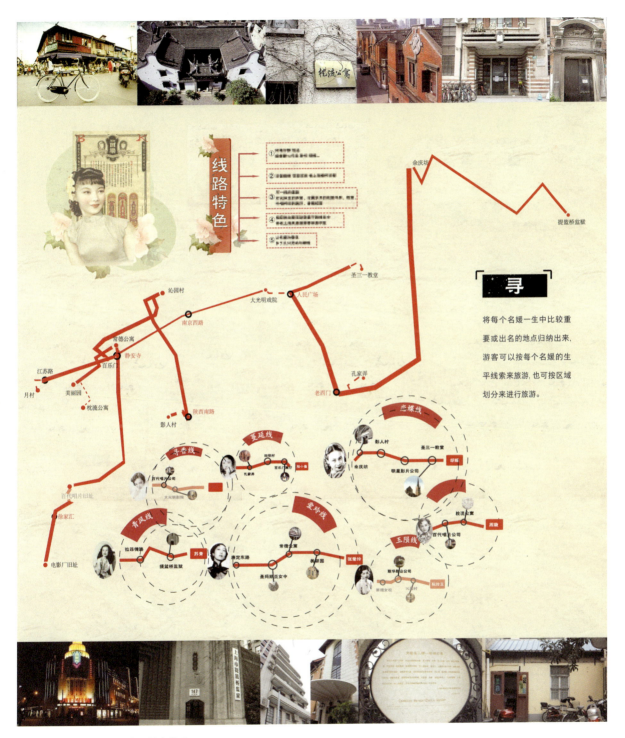

图2 "寻找玫瑰红"活动区域路线图

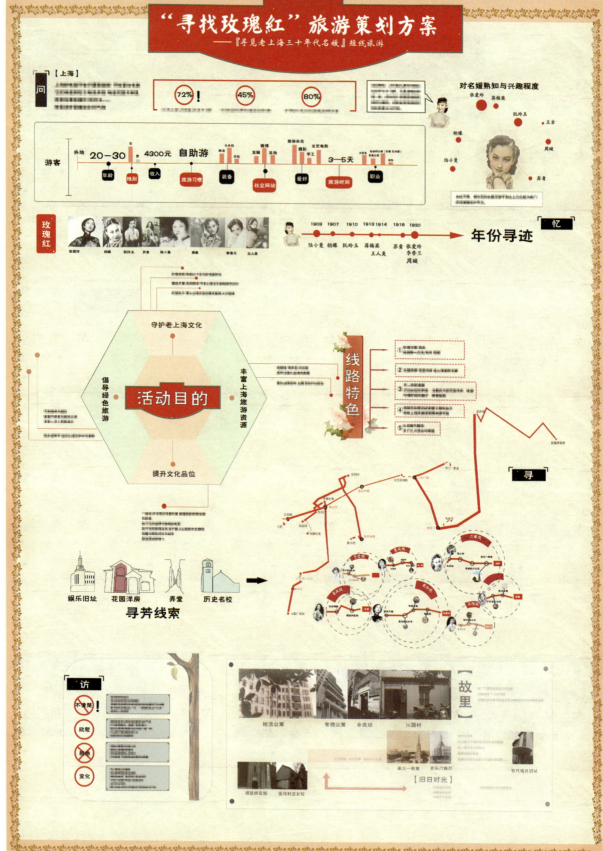

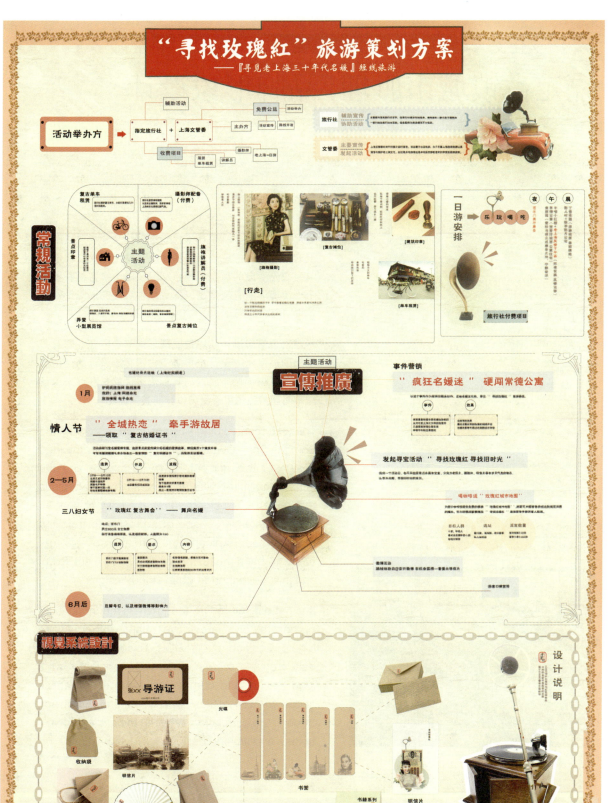

嘉定古镇城市肌理：品牌形象设计
THE TEXTURE OF JIADING ANCIENT TOWN: THE BRANDING DESIGN

作者姓名
张君如 Zhang Junru

作品形式
标志设计
视觉识别系统设计
Logo Design
Visual Identity System Design

指导教师
闵洁 Min Jie

嘉定古镇的城市肌理从宋代一直延续至今，对这座古镇的标志设计来说，城市肌理及其背后的人文价值，成为必先考虑的重要问题。从卫星图上很容易看到这个十字加环的有趣造型，探究这种肌理的形成是对嘉定古镇历史的溯源，也是标志设计的一个方向。

不难发现标志设计和城市肌理之间有着同源、同旨、互动的关系。本设计主要基于古镇标志设计的可持续性，通过古镇城市肌理与其标志设计的关联性来论证城市肌理特色运用于品牌设计的有效性。

The texture of Jiading Ancient Town has continued from the Song Dynasty to the present. For the logo design of this ancient town, its texture and the humanistic value have become an important issue that must be considered first. It's easy to see the town's interesting shape of a cross-ring from the satellite map. Exploring the formation of this texture is to trace the history of Jiading Ancient Town, and it is a direction to obtain logo design.

It is not difficult to find that there is a homologous, purposeful and interactive relationship between logo design and town texture. This design is mainly based on the sustainability of the ancient town's logo design, and demonstrates the effectiveness of the texture features applied in the brand design through the correlation between the ancient town's texture and its logo design.

图1 "嘉定古镇" 现存古迹

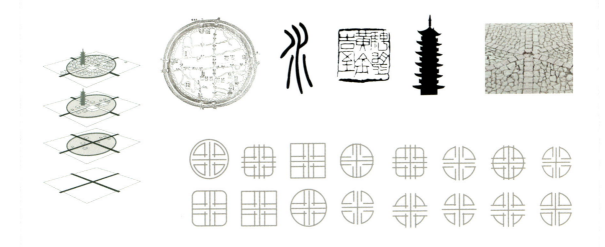

图2 "嘉定古镇"城市肌理中的古迹符号设计

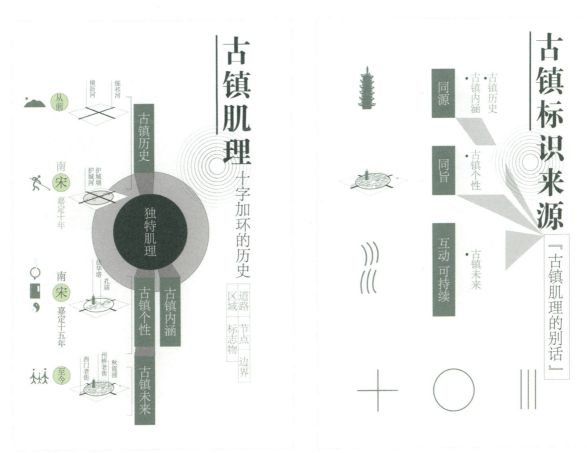

图3 "嘉定古镇"城市肌理与标志设计关系的信息设计图解

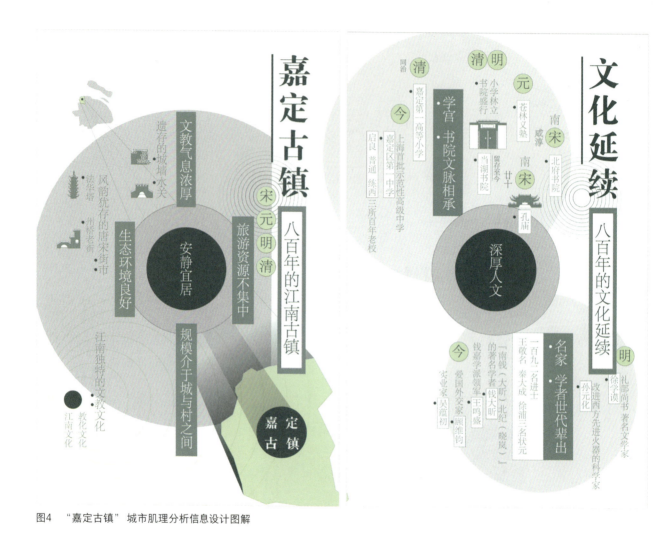

图4 "嘉定古镇"城市肌理分析信息设计图解

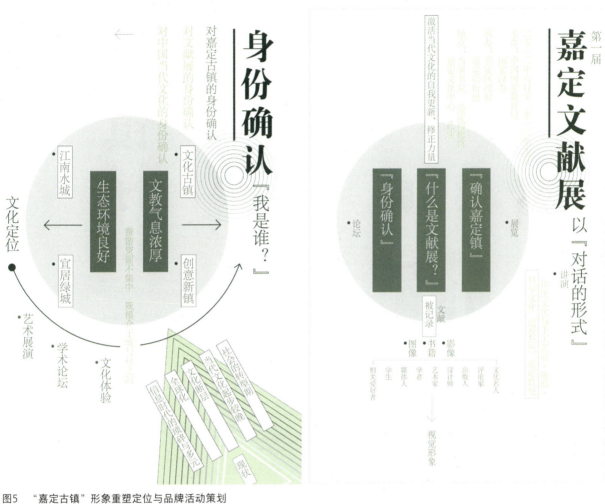

图5 "嘉定古镇"形象重塑定位与品牌活动策划

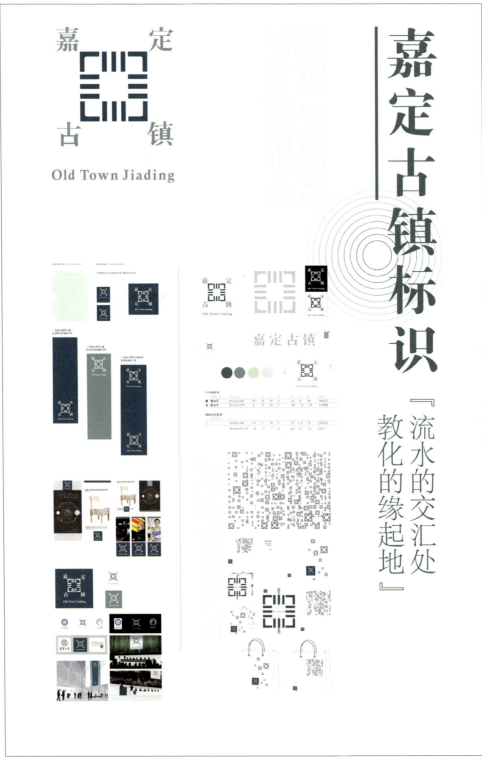

图6　"嘉定古镇"标识设计与应用

图7　"嘉定文献展"标识设计与应用

寻访巷陌: 杭州 "巷道文化" 商业推广

SEARCHING ALLEYS: COMMERCIAL PROMOTION OF "ALLEYWAY CULTURE" IN HANGZHOU

作者姓名
钱星原 Qian Xingyuan

作品形式
推广策划
品牌设计
Promotion Planning
Branding Design

指导教师
闵洁 Min Jie

本设计研究的是杭州城 "巷道文化" 的商业推广。在城市迅速发展的今天，一些老旧的建筑因为所处位置和功能不全成为城市发展的阻碍，原本生活其中的人，被迫离开了这个圈子。

杭州的巷道文化诞生于市井之中，代表了地方文化的延续，如果说西湖是以文人审美导向而获得了美名，那么杭州城的巷道则代表了素颜杭州与草根文化的缩影，诗歌、民谣等艺术都在巷道这个媒介中彼此依存。此设计所寻求的是一种人文遗产和现代生活相共存的方式，让巷道成为一个被关注的话题，并挖掘其延伸的可能性。

This project is the study of the commercial promotion of "Alleyway Culture" in Hangzhou. Today, with the rapid development of the city, some old buildings have become obstacles to the development of the city due to their locations and incomplete functions, and the people who used to live in old buildings are forced to leave the circle.

The alleyway culture of Hangzhou, born in the city life, represents the continuation of local culture. If West Lake gains its reputation from the aesthetic orientation of literati, then the alleyway in Hangzhou represents Hangzhou without makeup, the epitome of grass-roots culture, poetry and folk songs are all in the alley and depend on each other. This design seeks a way of humanistic heritage coexisting with modern life, making the alleyway a topic of concern and exploring the possibility of its extension.

图1 "巷道文化" 策划推广海报设计

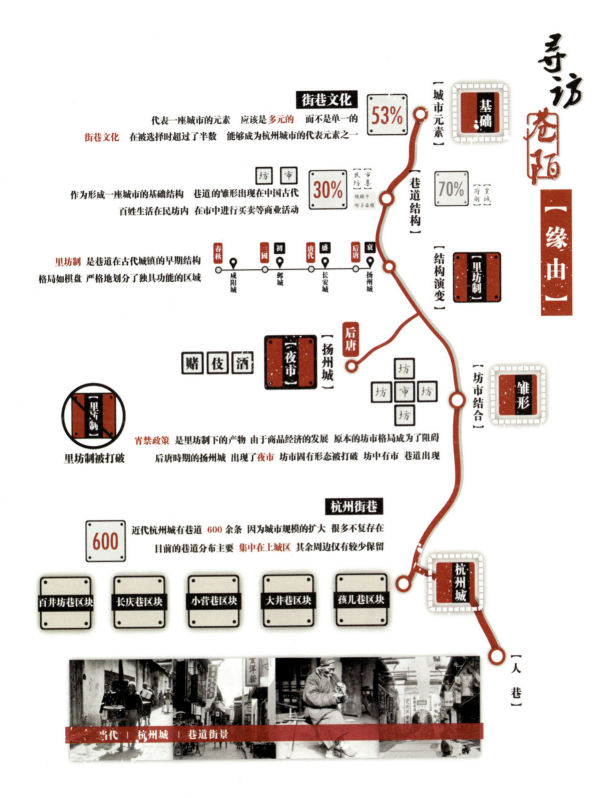

寻访巷陌【缘由】

街巷文化

代表一座城市的元素　应该是**多元的**　而不是单一的
街巷文化　在被选择时超过了半数　能够成为杭州城市的代表元素之一

53%　【城市元素】　【基础】

作为形成一座城市的基础结构　巷道的雏形出现在中国古代
百姓生活在民坊内　在市中进行买卖等商业活动

坊　市　**30%**　【民坊】【市集】城镇中所占面积　【巷道结构】

70%　【皇城】【府街】

里坊制是巷道在古代城镇的早期结构
格局如棋盘　严格地划分了独具功能的区域

春秋　三国　唐代　盛　后唐　衰
咸阳城　邺城　长安城　扬州城

【结构演变】　【里坊制】

赌　伎　酒　【夜市】【扬州城】后唐

坊　坊　市　坊　坊　【坊市结合】　【雏形】

里坊制被打破

宵禁政策是里坊制下的产物　由于商品经济的发展　原本的坊市格局成为了阻碍
后唐时期的扬州城　出现了**夜市**　坊市固有形态被打破　坊中有市　巷道出现

杭州街巷

600　近代杭州城有巷道 **600** 余条　因为城市规模的扩大　很多不复存在
目前的巷道分布主要　**集中在上城区**　其余周边仅有较少保留

百井坊巷区块　长庆巷区块　小营巷区块　大井巷区块　孩儿巷区块　【杭州城】

当代｜杭州城｜巷道街景　【人巷】

图2　"寻访巷道"策划前期分析信息设计图解

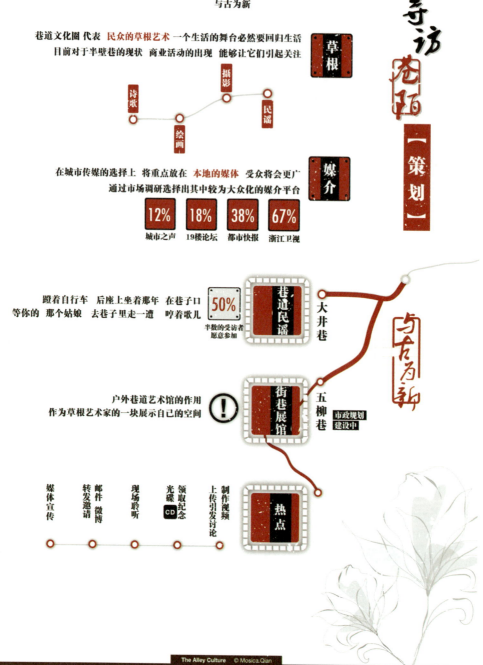

这里原本就是百姓草根艺术的舞台

乘之愈往　识之愈真　如将不尽

与古为新

寻访巷陌【策划】

巷道文化圈 代表 **民众的草根艺术** 一个生活的舞台必然要回归生活

目前对于半壁巷的现状 商业活动的出现 能够让它们引起关注

草根

诗歌　摄影　绘画　民谣

在城市传媒的选择上 将重点放在 **本地的媒体** 受众将会更广

通过市场调研选择出其中较为大众化的媒介平台

媒介

12%	18%	38%	67%
城市之声	19楼论坛	都市快报	浙江卫视

蹬着自行车　后座上坐着那年　在巷子口

等你的　那个姑娘　去巷子里走一遭　哼着歌儿

50%

半数的受访者愿意参加

巷道民谣

大井巷

与古为新

户外巷道艺术馆的作用

作为草根艺术家的一块展示自己的空间

(!)

街巷展馆

五柳巷

市政规划建设中

媒体宣传　邮件 微博　转发邀请　现场聆听　领取纪念 光碟 CD　制作视频 上传引发讨论

热点

The Alley Culture © Mosica.Qian

图3 "巷道文化"策划信息设计图解

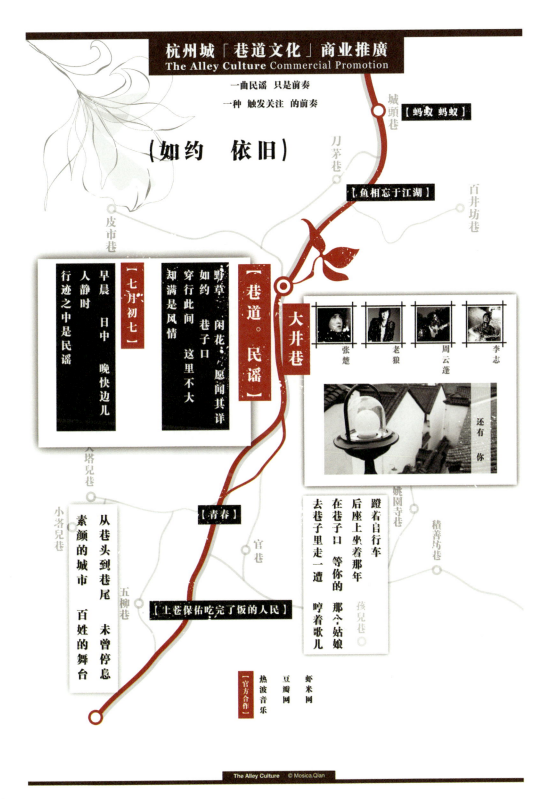

图4　"巷道文化"策划信息设计图解

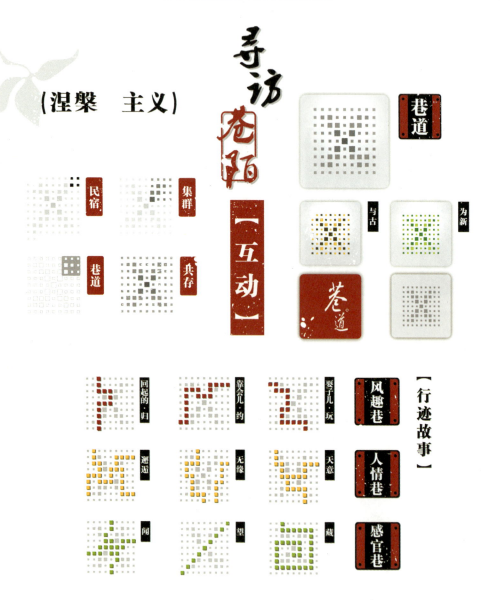

图5 "巷道文化"策划互动符号设计

杭州城「巷道文化」商业推广
The Alley Culture Commercial Promotion

【半壁巷】

希望着　是换颜重现

一等再等　拆着拆着

拆了半壁　却剩下另一半

半壁残垣

孤独地杵在那里

未知的命运　显然不容乐观

【行动】

【半壁巷】

Focus on
the BAN BI XIANG

【辰光】

【顾阊其详】

【特為蜀套】

巷道

【寻常巷陌　堪寻访】

图6　"巷道文化"视觉推广手册

数据之眼

VISUAL IDENTITY FOR "DATA, THROUGH THE EYE OF THE LENS" ART EXHIBITION

作者姓名

王琛 Chen Wang

作品形式

品牌策划

视觉设计

Branding promotion

Visual Design

数字成像的过程也是获取、传播和转换信息的过程。人类能够感知到的物理信号是自然界很小的一部分，而人类能看到的图像只是人类感知范围内的算法成像规律。在传感器和数字技术的帮助下，镜头后面的成像极大拓展了人类的生活经验；而人工智能领域里的图像识别与视觉语义生成原理，以及机器感知和人类感知的差异不仅是科技要探讨的主题，也是人文学科要探讨的主题。"数据之眼"是一场数据可视化摄影艺术展。展览标识使用一组数字符号来构建四个汉字的组成部分，并用这些数字符号和黑色背景色来暗示摄影镜头背后的成像原理和由此产生的深刻思考。

The process of digital imaging is also the process of acquiring, disseminating and transforming information. The physical signals that humans can perceive are a very small part of nature, and the images that humans can see are only the algorithm within the range of human perception. With the help of sensors and digital technology, the imaging behind the lens greatly expands the human experience of life. The principles of image recognition and visual semantic generation in the field of artificial intelligence, as well as the difference between machine perception and human perception, are not only topics to be discussed in science and technology, but also topics in humanities. "Data, Through the eye of the lens" is a data visualization photography art exhibition. The exhibition logo uses a set of digital symbols to construct the components of the four Chinese characters, and uses these digital symbols and black background color to allude to the imaging principle behind the photographic lens and the resulting deep thinking.

图1   "数据之眼"字体设计概念草图

图2   "数据之眼"设计应用

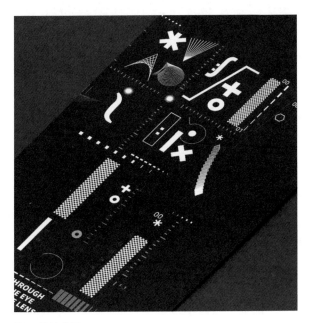

图3 设计应用

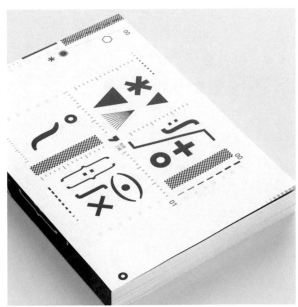

图4 设计应用

图5 设计应用

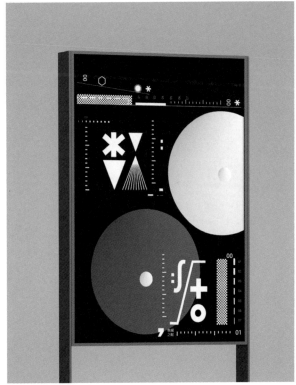

图6 设计应用

B/
03

—

互联网类

洛杉矶艺术步行街

DOWNTOWN LA ARTWALK REBRANDING AND NAVIGATION SYSTEM

作者姓名
艾琳 · 林 Irene Lin

作品形式
品牌策划 视觉设计
导航系统
Planning / Visual Design
Navigation System

指导教师
王琛 Chen Wang

图1 APP 设计界面

Downtown LA Artwalk 是洛杉矶市中心每月一次的艺术活动，旨在宣传40多家画廊，以及周边的餐厅、酒吧和数百家艺术家驻场工作室。品牌战略强调数字服务的创新解决方案。数据可视化将在信息搜索、过滤、导航、行程规划等方面发挥关键作用，使设计能够利用直观的界面、良好的交互反应和简洁的信息来提升用户体验。

产品功能将侧重于信息整合的概念，分类和过滤众多的画廊数据，根据用户需求生成个性化解决方案与个性化地图，方便查看、查找、过滤、更新、共享信息和导航。导航大型数据集需要新的范式，这些范式超越了查找和消费内容的典型技术，同时提高了可用性和参与度。出于这个原因，我相信在线环境中设计的未来是数据可视化，它不仅仅将被用于分析目的，更将用于内容发现。换句话说，数据可视化将成为界面。

Downtown LA Artwalk is a monthly art event in downtown Los Angeles that promotes 40+ galleries, as well as surrounding restaurants, bars and hundreds of artist-in-residence studios. The brand strategy is emphasised on innovational solution for digital service. Data visualization will play a key role in information search, filtering, navigation, and itinerary planning, so that the design can use an intuitive interface, good interactive reaction, and relavent information to enhance user's experience.

Product functions will focus on the concept of information integration, classification and filtering of large amounts of gallery data, generation of personalized solutions according to user needs, personalized maps to facilitate viewing, finding, filtering, updating, sharing information and navigation. Navigating large datasets calls for new paradigms that extend beyond the typical techniques of finding and consuming content, while increasing both usability and engagement. For that reason, data visualization in the online context is used not only for analytic purposes, but rather for content discovery. In other words, data visualization becomes the interface.

图2 洛杉矶市区 摄影：王琛

1. The Revolution

2. Categorized by Time

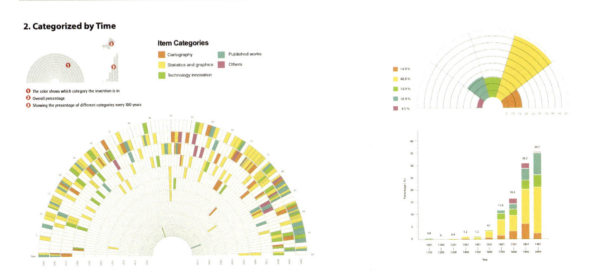

图3 在研究阶段进行的可视化方法分析：将十个世纪以来与数据可视化相关的制图、
统计图表、技术和书籍创新按时间、地点和图形类别归类。 这些里程碑通过不同的颜
色编码与对应的国家/地区联系起来，并运用到项目的问题和数码情境中

图4　在研究阶段进行的可视化方法分析：可视化
创新与地区的关系以及在不同时期的发展

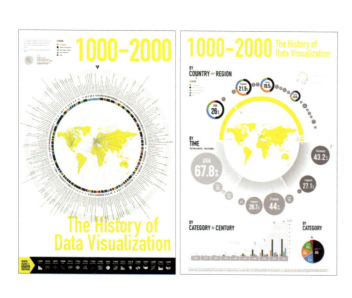

图5　在研究阶段进行的可视化方法分析：将一千年来
与数据可视化相关的制图、统计图表、技术和书籍创
新按时间、地点和图形类别归类

图6　从用户调查中得知，电子服务计划的主要问
题是信息量庞杂，用户无法快速吸收和规划出游计
划。因此，为了提供一种直观的方式来显示画廊
和艺术品之间的关系和自我组织，规划数据变得
至关重要

图7 将可视化方法运用到数字产品中，测试不同的信息组合和导航方式，增加互动体验

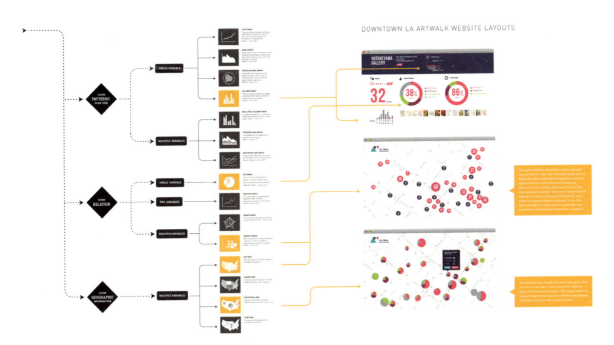

图8 将在研究阶段总结的可视化方法运用到项目的情境中

GRID SYSTEM

The grid system is based on the triangle shape of the logotype.

ICONS

The icons are utilized on the websites and print publication.

FILTER	RESTAURANT	BAR	MAP	REVIEW

ARTWORK MEDIA	ARTWORK STYLE	GALLERY HOURS	GALLERY

SKETCHES

图9 品牌与UI设计

图10 手机UI界面

图11 Logo设计

THIS IS A MULTIPLE GALLERIES VISIT
PLANNER WEBSITE. IT VISUALLY
INTEGRATES MAP, ART WORKS AND
TIME, AND THROUGH DIFFERENT
FILTERS EFFICIENTLY HELPING YOU
DESIGN A ONE-DAY TRIP OF VISITING
YOUR SELECTED GALLERIES IN
DOWNTOWN LA. YOU CAN SHARE
THE FINISHED MAP TO YOUR FRIENDS
AS AN INVITATION FOR THE TRIP.

Select your prefered visit date

The user can choose the date
for visiting the galleries in the
begining. However, the user can
still change the date later.

图12 画廊、艺术场所和餐饮业数据的可视化界面帮助用户进行分析推
理，以支持用户的决策过程，使他们能够对空间和量化信息进行比较和
交互

图13 手机UI界面

图14 洛杉矶市区   摄影：王琛

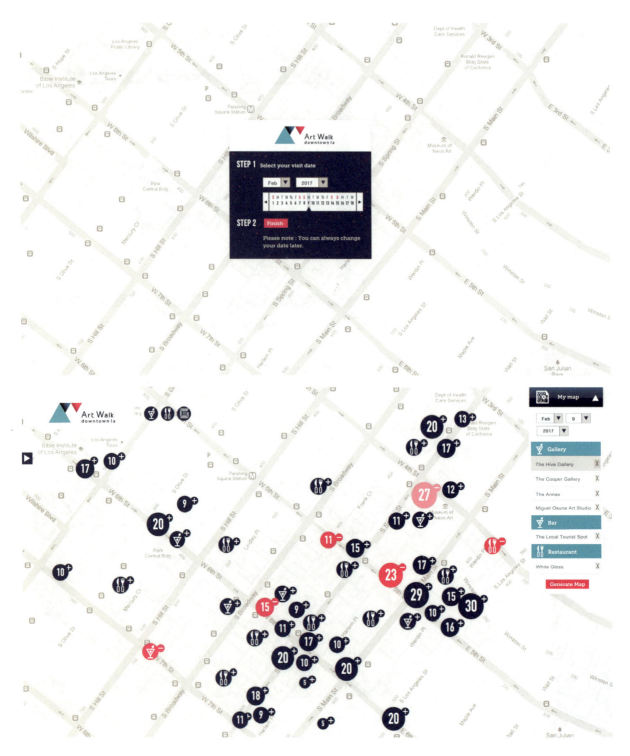

图15，16 网页UI界面

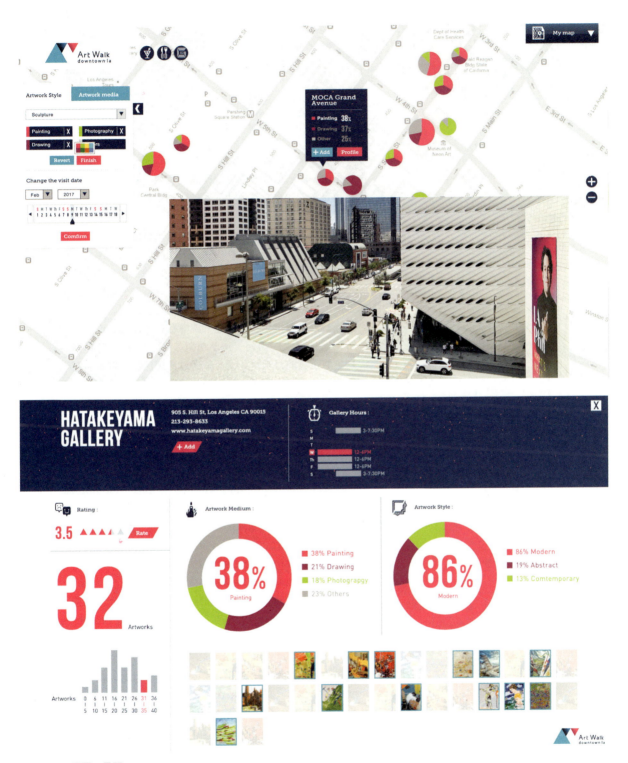

图17，18 网页UI界面

医疗系统客户管理系统

HEALTHCARE CUSTOMER RELATIONSHIP MANAGEMENTS SYSTEM OPTIMIZATION PLAN

作者姓名
希琳·伊萨德瓦斯塔 Shirin Isadvastar

作品形式
信息服务系统设计
用户体验设计
用户界面设计
Information Design
User Experience Design
User Interface Design

指导教师
王琛 Chen Wang
阿诺德·荷兰 Arnold Holland

图1 "设计目标与策略"图标

近年来，美国的医疗患者数量不断增加，而医疗资源却相对保持不变。解决医疗资源短缺问题的有效途径之一是提高医疗机构自身的效率。本设计项目的目的是改善医疗机构的客服管理系统的流通过程。设计者通过搜集现有的客户信息管理系统，收集医疗代理人、医生和患者三方的反馈，分析信息组织结构和服务系统过程中存在的问题，然后从用户体验的角度调整信息的组织方式，去除了重复的操作步骤，简化用户界面，提高导航工具的直观性。设计者首先收集作为当前客户信息管理系统用户的医疗代理、医生和患者的反馈。通过分析信息架构和客户管理系统中存在的问题，设计人员能够解决信息组织问题、消除重复步骤、简化用户界面、提高导航工具的直观性。设计师通过梳理流通中的不合理设置，达到优化信息系统、提高系统效率的目的，从而提升医疗机构的品牌体验。

In recent years, the number of medical patients in the United States has continued to increase, while medical resources have remained relatively unchanged. One of the effective ways to address the problem of medical resources shortage is to improve the efficiency of the medical institutions itself. The purpose of this design project is to improve the circulation process of the information management system of medical institutions. The designer first collects the feedback from medical agents, doctors and patients through the current customer information management system. By analyzing the problems existing in the information archtecture and the custumer management system, designer able to address the information organization problems, elimilate repeated steps, simplify the user interface and improve the intuitiveness of the navigation tools. By sorting out the unreasonable settings in the circulation, the designer achieves the purpose of optimizing the information system and improving the efficiency of the system, thereby enhancing the brand experience of medical institutions.

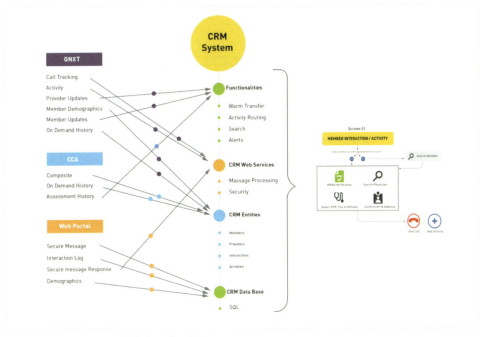

图2 客服管理系统构架与信息流通过程图解

图3 用户需求调研

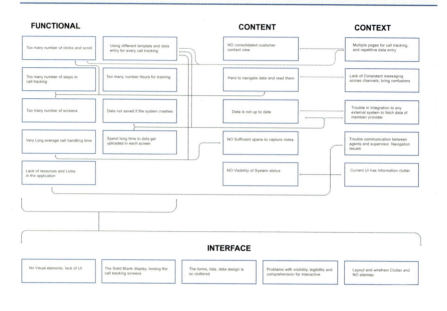

图4 CRM系统构架与信息流通过程分析

图5 用户图像与用户需求分析

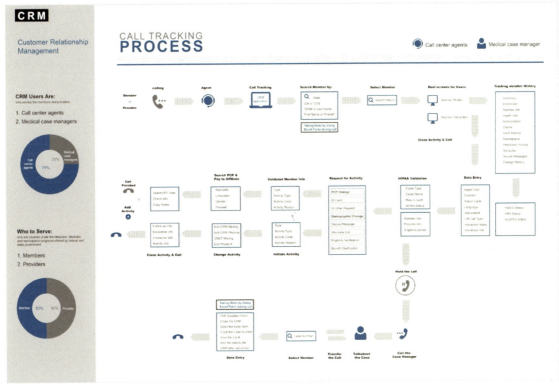

图6 CRM 系统的信息流程图

CURRENT UI CRM

Time	Search & Member profile	Search & Provider profile	All other request	ID Card request	Demographic Change	PCP Change Request	Welcome Call	Welcome Call with other task
⏱	6 min 59 sec	6min 25 sec	3 min	5 min 10 sec	7 min 30 sec	3 min 30 sec	1min 36 sec	2 hr 22 min

Clicks	Search & Member profile	Search & Provider profile	All other request	ID Card request	Demographic Change	PCP Change Request	Welcome Call	Welcome Call with other task
🖱	6	6	21	18	35	39	24	24+

Screens	Search & Member profile	Search & Provider profile	All other request	ID Card request	Demographic Change	PCP Change Request	Welcome Call	Welcome Call with other task
⛶	2	2	5	7	6	8	6	6+2

NEW UI CRM

Time	Search & Member profile	Search & Provider profile	All other request	ID Card request	Demographic Change	PCP Change Request	Welcome Call	Welcome Call with other task
⏱	34 sec	34 sec	46 sec	55 sec	1 min 55 sec	3 min 30 sec	36 sec	36 sec + 1min 55sec

Clicks	Search & Member profile	Search & Provider profile	All other request	ID Card request	Demographic Change	PCP Change Request	Welcome Call	Welcome Call with other task
🖱	2	2	4	4	4	4	2	2+4

Screens	Search & Member profile	Search & Provider profile	All other request	ID Card request	Demographic Change	PCP Change Request	Welcome Call	Welcome Call with other task
⛶	1	1	1	1	1	1	1	1

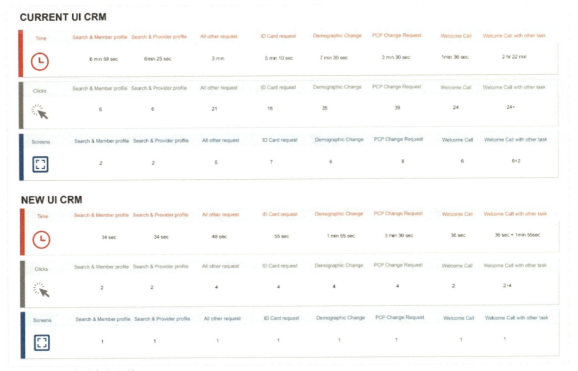

图7 设计目标分析与评估

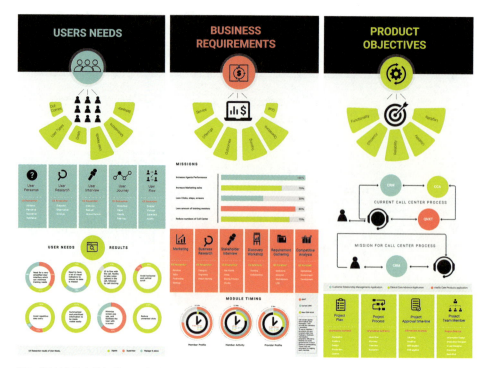

图8 设计过程中的视觉呈现方法

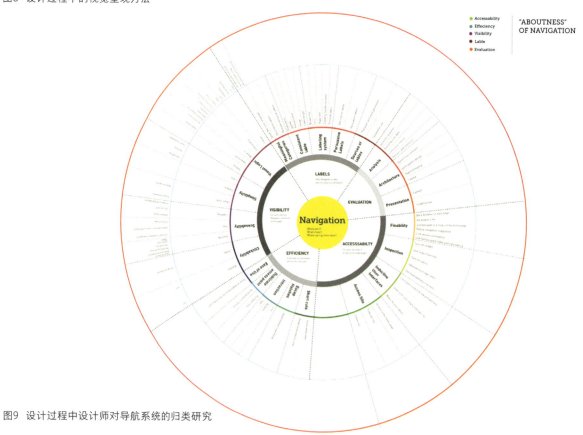

图9 设计过程中设计师对导航系统的归类研究

图10 设计师将设计过程整理成册

图11 对设计效果的评估

神裔：神话主题桌游品牌设计

GOD'S DESCENDANTS: BRANDING DESIGN OF TRADITIONAL CHINNESE MYTHOLOGY ADAPTATION CARD GAME

作者姓名

王旗 Wang Qi

刘超奇 Liu Chaoqi

作品形式

品牌策划

视觉设计

Branding Design

Visual Design

指导教师

闵洁 Min Jie

本项目意在提炼网络玄幻文学的核心源泉中国传统神话，将最古老的中国神话以现代网络小说的语境风格进行再创意，并使其归纳入同一个世界观架构之下。

设计选择桌面卡牌游戏作为世界观具象化的体现，运用水墨、书法、白描这三种传统艺术手法，并与当代设计风格融合，试图在内容为王的"互联网+"时代探索文创产品生态的一种新型途径。

This project aims to extract the core source of online fantasy literature, to recreate the oldest Chinese mythology in the context of modern online novels, and to summarize it under the same worldview framework.

The design chooses the tabletop card game as the embodiment of world view, using three traditional artistic techniques of ink painting, calligraphy and line drawing, and integrated with the contemporary design style. It is a new way to explore the ecology of cultural and creative products in the Internet + era in which content is king.

图1，2 "神裔"桌游IP内容衍生创意设计

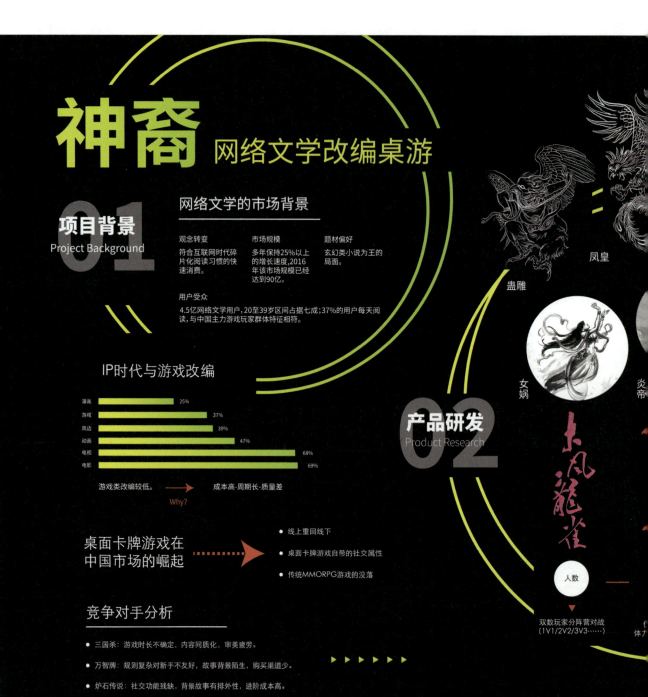

神裔
网络文学改编桌游

01 项目背景
Project Background

网络文学的市场背景

观念转变
符合互联网时代碎片化阅读习惯的快速消费。

市场规模
多年保持25%以上的增长速度,2016年该市场规模已经达到90亿。

题材偏好
玄幻类小说为王的局面。

用户受众
4.5亿网络文学用户,20至39岁区间占据七成;37%的用户每天阅读,与中国主力游戏玩家群体特征相符。

IP时代与游戏改编

- 漫画 25%
- 游戏 37%
- 周边 39%
- 动画 47%
- 电视 68%
- 电影 69%

游戏类改编较低。 → 成本高-周期长-质量差

Why?

桌面卡牌游戏在中国市场的崛起

- 线上重回线下
- 桌面卡牌游戏自带的社交属性
- 传统MMORPG游戏的没落

竞争对手分析

- 三国杀:游戏时长不确定,内容同质化,审美疲劳。
- 万智牌:规则复杂对新手不友好,故事背景陌生,购买渠道少。
- 炉石传说:社交功能残缺,背景故事有排外性,进阶成本高。

02 产品研发
Product Research

蛊雕

凤皇

女娲

炎帝

木风龙雀

人数

双数玩家分阵营对战
(1V1/2V2/3V3……)

图3 "神裔"桌游IP内容衍生创意设计图解

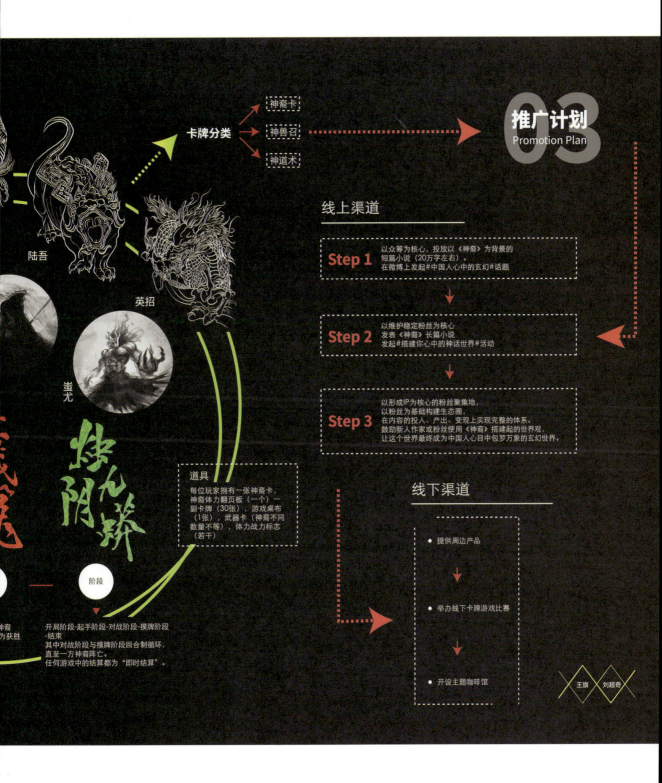

卡牌分类 → 神裔卡
卡牌分类 → 神兽召
卡牌分类 → 神道术

陆吾

英招

蚩尤

03 推广计划
Promotion Plan

线上渠道

Step 1 以众筹为核心，投放以《神裔》为背景的短篇小说（20万字左右）。
在微博上发起#中国人心中的玄幻#话题

Step 2 以维护稳定粉丝为核心
发表《神裔》长篇小说
发起#搭建你心中的神话世界#活动

Step 3 以形成IP为核心的粉丝聚集地，
以粉丝为基础构建生态圈，
在内容的投入、产出、变现上实现完整的体系。
鼓励新人作家或粉丝使用《神裔》搭建起的世界观，
让这个世界最终成为中国人目中包罗万象的玄幻世界。

道具
每位玩家拥有一张神裔卡，
神裔体力翻页板（一个）一
副卡牌（30张），游戏桌布
（1张），武器卡（神裔不同
数量不等），体力战力标志
（若干）

阶段

神裔
为获胜

开局阶段-起手阶段-对战阶段-摸牌阶段
-结束
其中对战阶段与摸牌阶段回合制循环，
直至一方神裔阵亡。
任何游戏中的结算都为"即时结算"。

线下渠道

● 提供周边产品

● 举办线下卡牌游戏比赛

● 开设主题咖啡馆

王旗 刘超奇

GoFun: 移动社交旅行APP用户体验设计

GOFUN: MOBBILE SOCIAL TRAVEL APP USER EXPERIENCE DESIGN

作者姓名
陈珍雅 Chen Zhenya

作品形式
交互界面设计
品牌策划
信息设计
Interactive Interface Design
Branding Planning
Information Design

指导教师
闵洁 Min Jie

随着移动设备的普及，APP的运用也越加广泛。本次针对"GoFun"社交旅行APP的研究主要分为用户体验设计及前期推广策划两部分。设计通过对旅行APP的市场调查及用户群体调查厘清现有社交旅行APP的优劣势，从而为"GoFun"品牌APP做以下三方面的用户体验设计：基于地理信息系统的互动交流设计；移动设备与社交旅行APP的功能结合设计；UGC的运用设置。同时，制定"GoFun"社交旅行APP的前期推广宣传。

With the popularity of mobile devices, the use of APP is also more extensive. This research on the "GoFun" social travel APP is mainly divided into two parts: user experience design and early promotion planning. Through market research on travel APP and user group survey, it is expected to clarify the advantages and disadvantages of existing social travel APPs, so as to make user experience design for the "GoFun" social travel APP in three aspects: interactive communication design based on geographic information system; functional combination design of mobile devices and social travel APP; UGC application settings. Meanwile, the "GoFun" social travel APP is developed for early promotion.

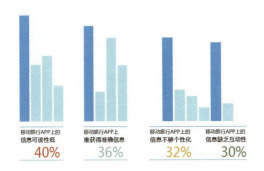

移动旅行APP上的信息可读性低 **40%**　移动旅行APP上难获得准确信息 **36%**　移动旅行APP上的信息不够个性化 **32%**　移动旅行APP上的信息缺乏互动性 **30%**

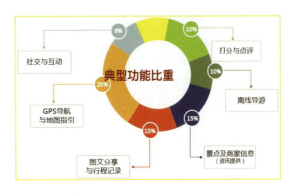

典型功能比重

社交与互动 9%
打分与点评 10%
GPS导航与地图指引 25%
离线导游 10%
景点及商家信息（资讯提供）15%
图文分享与行程记录 15%

可伸缩的交互式地图

扫描式的区域信息地图

互动式的串联足迹图

图1　"GoFun"移动社交旅行APP界面设计

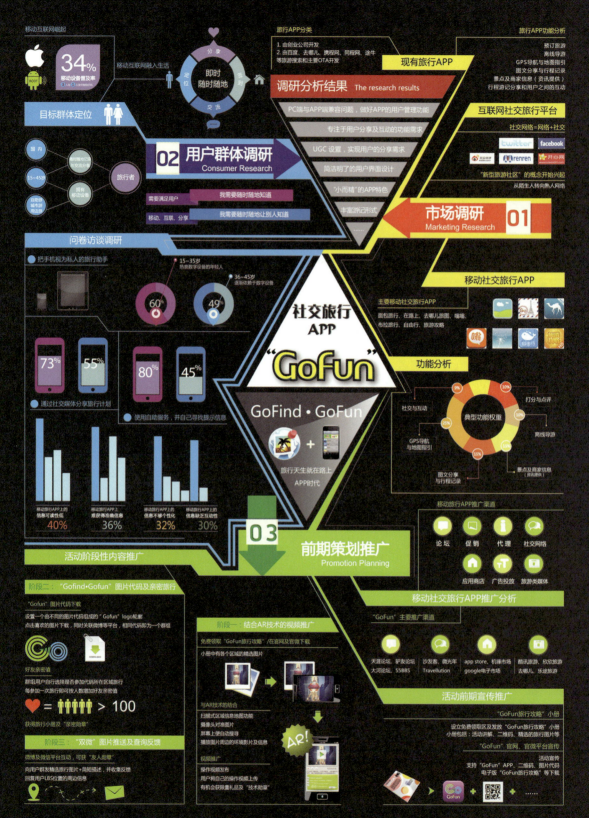

图2 "GoFun"移动社交旅行APP用户体验信息设计图解

"GoFun"（行趣）移动社交旅行APP 用户体验及界面设计

GoFun

设计说明：

图形：根据"GoFun"的理念、用户体验要求及界面设计进行了以下设计。标志图形的灵感来自于єℓ不的设计过程，旨在突出本款APP的刚度动力及交流方式。大量采用圆环图形由表灵现代意象同以及旅游的情境标示，句为可增山之me山峰，突出旅行的灵象。组合成"Go"的式样，以及中间部分的小small标针，表达出移动与旅行出发的理念，圆环嵌入以环境的感受，进一步突出了顺畅生动交流之意。

字体："GoFun"采用英文字体，一起不以"行趣"出现。同时根据环境的圆形感觉对字体进行设计。

用色：主要以黄绿色为生，根据旅行给人的感觉，选取绿色的黄绿蓝色系，表达一种清新生动。

用户体验设计标准

定位及诉求点
定位：国内移动社交旅行的第三方应用程序
诉求点：便捷、即时、简洁、交流

用户综合体验标准
用户界面简洁性、导航清晰
图文间的一致性
页面下载速度快
内容的丰富性
操作的便捷性

功能设定
GPS导航与地图指引（15%）
图文分享与行程记录（25%）
社交与互动（35%）
离线使用（10%）
其他（15%）

可伸缩的交互式地图

可切换插画版及实图版，路线信息示足迹地图即可查看。图片GPS位置记录身有地图链接，点击查看周边信息

结合AR技术

使用"GoFun"的AR技术，将手机对准纸媒图片，即可播放各图片没有呈现的细节影片

AR技术的视频形式
制作AR技术完美呈现的视频，以极具创意和高端科技感的展示形式作为营销策略

互动式的串联足迹图

记录照片的GPS位置，关联微博微信等社交平台，可分享照片并生成足迹地图及带时间轴的照片墙

基于地理信息系统的互动交流设计

扫描式的区域信息地图

将照相镜头对准四周环境，根据环境自动判断位置，屏幕显示附近的主要信息。扫描区域500米至30公里。显示周边景点方位及距离

移动设备与社交旅行APP的功能结合设计

UGC的运用设置

GoFind·GoFun 行趣

语音（可听）
选语音解说频道
多种方言可选

景点语音解说

行程摘报语音模式
录制行程心情的语音，配上心情表情发表
可关联微信等平台分享

关联熟人旅行社区

同步"GoFun"
在微博等平台上添加好友，与好友制定的旅行计划、好友的点评和分享，以上都可反向同步至"GoFun"，还可以向好友们"求攻略"

"路书"明信片
用户拍摄的旅程"路书"
可制成精美的明信片发布到APP，关联到相应的位置立即分享验好友，好友可以发布"喜欢""分享"等指令

互动（可交流）

"UP or DOWN"
UP or DOWN（往上/下的大拇指）
回应肯定与否
可以进行收藏、分享及跟贴评论

PC端与APP同步管理个人信息

同步信息登录
用户登录信息=社交名片
可另注册，可从其他平台帐号登录后随时切换模式

视频（可看）

发布旅程
可通过相机拍摄旅程
关联其他社交平台发布视频

离线记录
无信号时利用"离线记录"功能保存拍摄位置

旅行记录标签，添加关键词等旅行后在PC端添加详实描述对撰写做辅述，提供点评功能

PC端与APP可共同转换

B/
04

—

健康环保类

Quake: 加州抗震应急服务设计方案

QUAKE: EARTHQUAKE EMERGENCY SERVICE DESIGN PLAN

作者姓名
周凌宇 Lingyu Zhou

作品形式
信息系统设计
品牌设计
Information System Design
Branding Design

指导教师
王琛
Chen Wang
塞尔希奥·利扎拉加
Sergio Lizarraga

Quake抗震应急服务设计方案是对加州政府推动的主体抗震方案的补充和延展。本方案利用USGS Science for a changing world 网站的地震数据可视化了加州众多的地质断层分布带和170多年中地震发生的频率，以警醒加州居民居安思危。同时，方案针对加州文化族裔多元、语言不同的特点，提出将抗震知识的推广以及抗震应急设施的布置融入社区文化建设，用审慎的态度与有效的预防积极构建成熟的社区抗震体系。

Quake earthquake emergency service design plan is a supplement and extension to the main earthquake resistance plan promoted by the California government. This project uses the Earthquakes data of the USGS (Science for a changing world) website to visualize the distribution of numerous geological faults in California and the frequency of earthquakes over the past 170 years, so as to alert California residents to be prepared for danger. Meanwhile, due to the facts of diverse cultures and ethnic groups, and different languages, the plan proposes to integrate the promotion of earthquake resistance knowledge and the distrubition of facilities into the construction of community culture, and actively build a mature community seismic system.

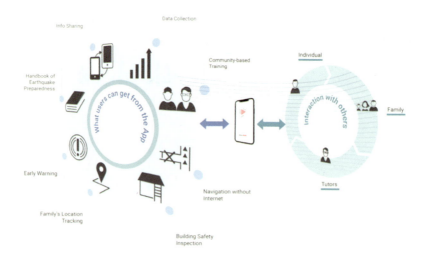

图1 设计方案流程图

GEOLOGICAL FEATURES **AND** HUMANITY ENVIRONMENT **IN CALIFORNIA**

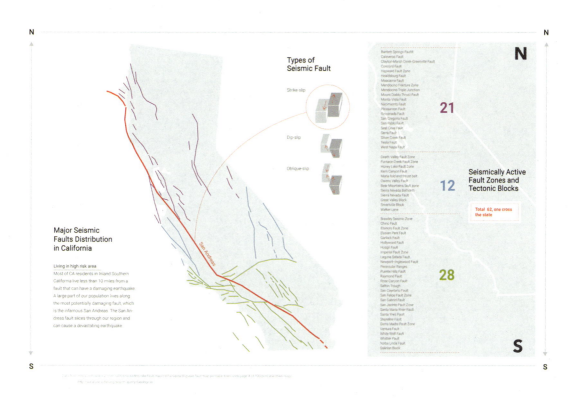

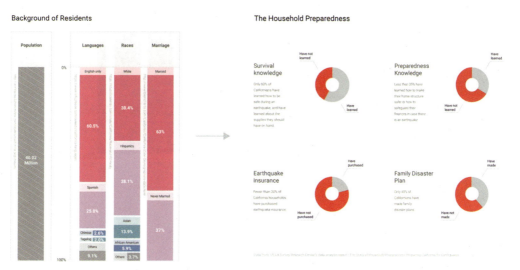

图2 加州地质特征与人文环境分析

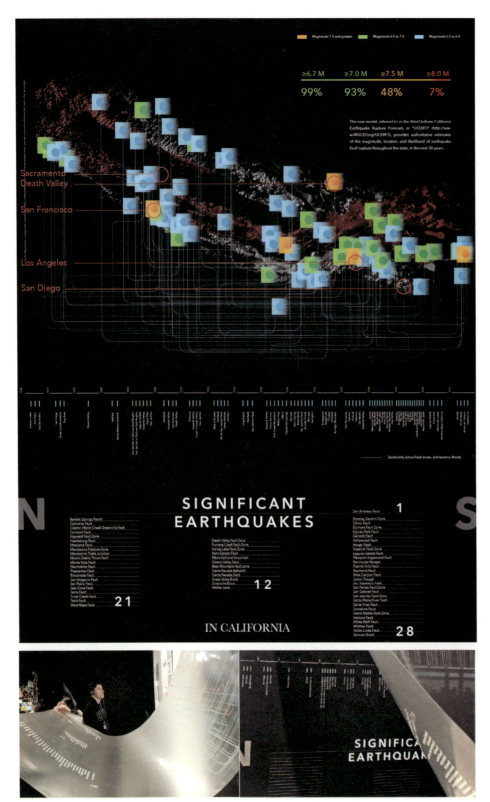

图3 地震和断层分布数据可视化研究，打印版海报通过信息分层和交互行为来提升阅读体验

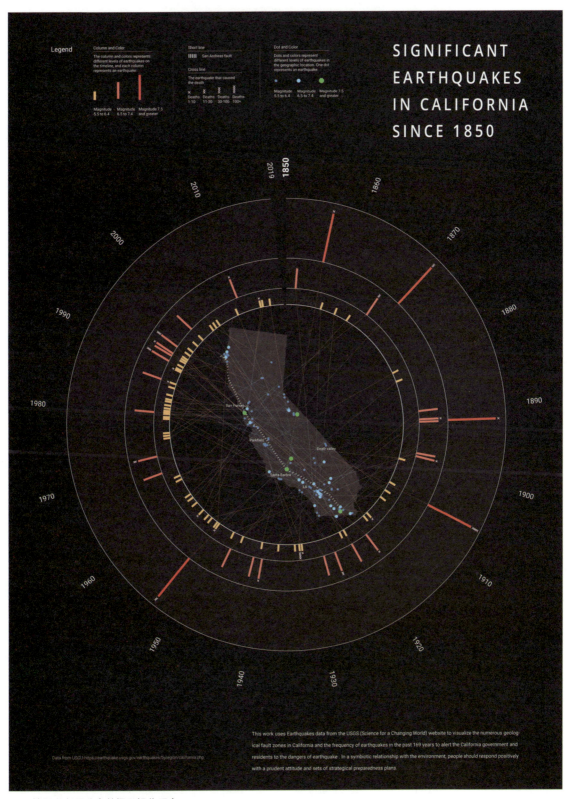

图4 地震和断层分布数据可视化研究

图5 服务流程图

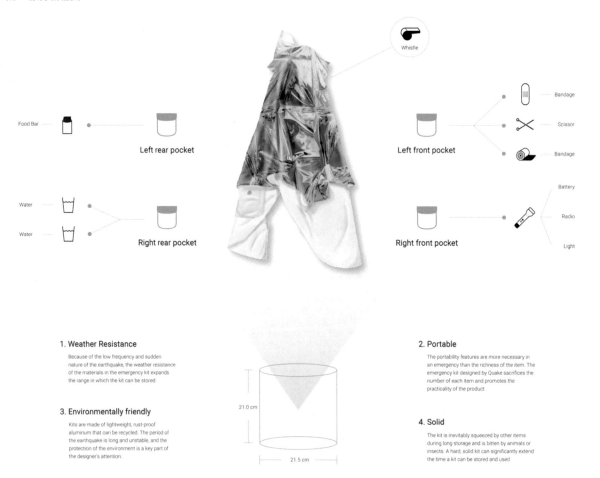

图6 地震应急包的设计

图7　用户测试应急包

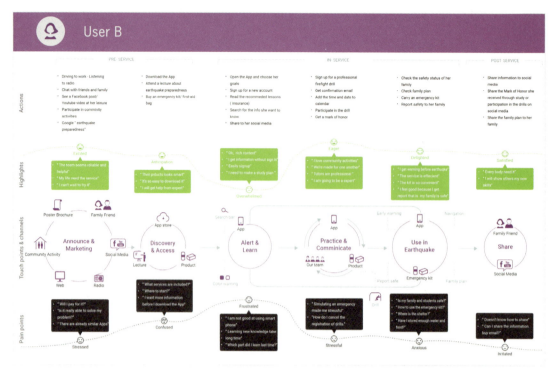

图8 用户体验调查

图9 Quake品牌视觉设计

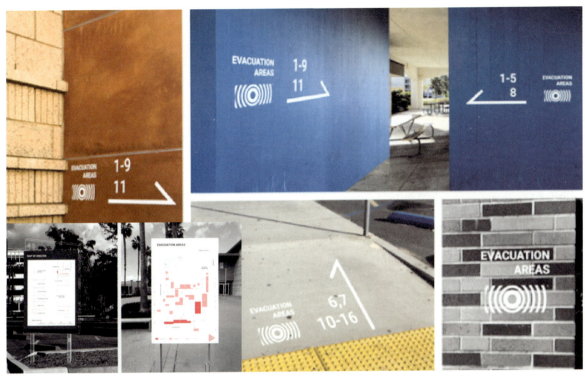

图10 社区防震设施信息设计

Earthquake Data

Quake warns of earthquakes that are occurring in California, and it also shows major earthquakes that happened in California history.

Navigation

Quake provides offline navigation services that allow users to find the nearest shelter, hospital, police station, fire station when they lose the mobile signal after an earthquake.

Emergency Model

Once the early warning system detects a major earthquake nearby, the emergency model will automatically pop up. Users can ask for help at one click, they can also view the family disaster plan that has been made, or track the location of family members before the earthquake.

Information Sharing

Information sharing can not only help people around you survive in the earthquake, but also create and expand a benign social circle to promote people's deepening understanding of the earthquake.

图11 移动应用程序界面设计

DTB: 用户体验与用户界面设计
DUMP THE BUMP USER EXPERIENCE & USER INTERFACE DESIGN

作者姓名
王琛 Chen Wang
瑞安·哈姆 Ryan Hamm
玛格丽特·齐斯克 Margaret Zisk
竺佳妮 Jiani Zhu

作品形式
用户体验设计
用户界面设计
User Experience Design
User Interface Design

Dump the Bump 是一款专为 WIC 项目[1]的产期妇女设计的手机应用程序。该应用程序允许用户在手机上记录和监督自己的体重、营养和情绪，并获取保持身体、心理和情绪健康的信息。设计师团队通过用户调研了解用户的生活方式和痛点，并以此为出发点分析用户行为。一款友好易用的手机应用程序可以融入用户的生活，成为用户管理个人信息的有效工具，并帮助用户建立平衡的生活方式，保持健康的习惯。

Dump the Bump is a mobile app designed for pregnant women in the WIC program. The app allows users to record and monitor their weight, nutrition and mood on their phone, and access information to maintain physical, mental and emotional health. The designer team understands the user's lifestyle and pain points through user research, and uses this as a starting point to analyze user behavior. A friendly and easy-to-use mobile application can be integrated into user's life, become an effective tool for user to manage personal information, and help user to establish a balanced lifestyle and maintain healthy habits.

----

1   WIC是加州政府为中低收入家庭的妇女和儿童提供的资助计划，资助范围包括食品、医疗和营养教育。

图1 移动应用程序的界面设计

图2 用户体验调研storyboard

图3 界面视觉元素

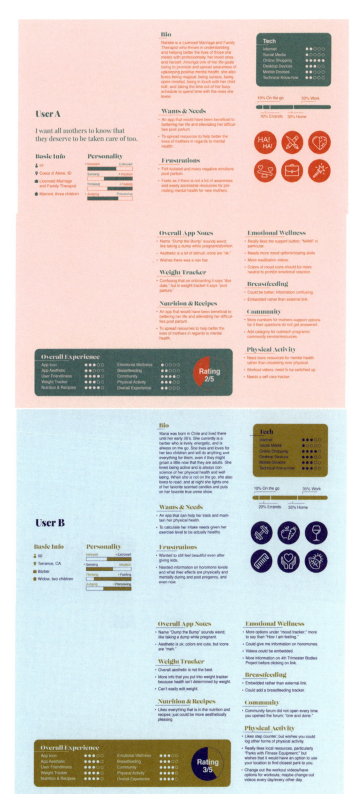

图4 用户体验调研

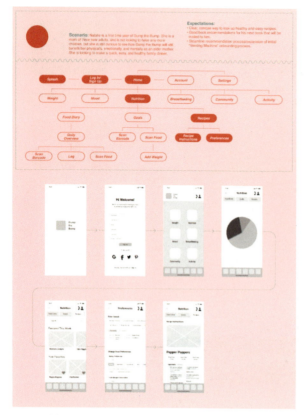

图5 用户场景

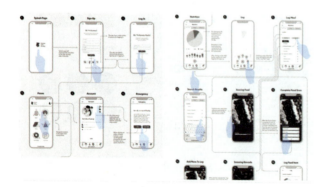

图6 用户调研

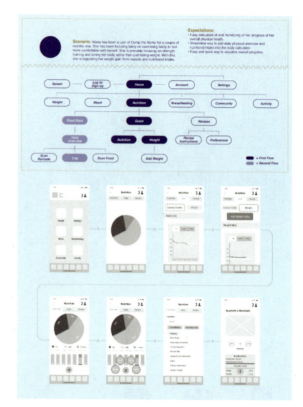

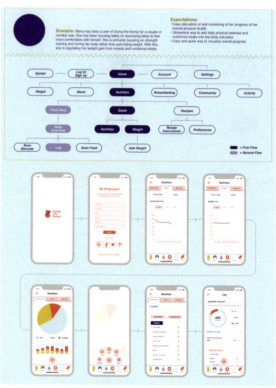

图7，8 用户场景

图9 界面设计

Identity and illustration

Use weight scale as a visual metaphor for weight measurement and remain balance of physical and mental wellness.

Blue: Considered to be middle-class color, it is trustworthy, reliable, calm, responsible and serenity.

RGB: #3300CC

RGB: #FF6633

Orange color is associated with meanings of joy, warmth, success, encouragement, change, determination, health, happiness, fun, enjoyment, and balance.

RGB: #FFCCFF

Peach represents human skin and human body. Also, it signifies a warm feeling of friendship and caring.

Key words:

Postpartum App
WIC Moms
return to
pre-pregnancy weight.

Key words:

Exercises
Tracking
One-stop service

Key words:

Peaceful mindset
Balanced
Happy
Healthy
Confident Mom

图10 品牌设计元素

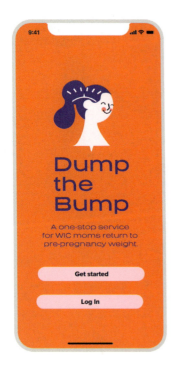

图11 品牌人物形象塑造

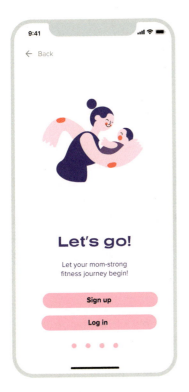

图12　界面设计

图13　品牌人物形象塑造

美国食物浪费调研与方案
FOOD WASTE IN USA

作者姓名
林孟昙 Meng Tan Lin

作品形式
信息设计
数据可视化
互动设计
Information Design
Data Visualization
Interaction Design

指导教师
王琛 Chen Wang

本项目试图通过数据分析证明，食物浪费是一个系统性问题，不仅与个人的行为和习惯有关，还受到自然环境、历史渊源、政策制定、文化传统和技术发展的影响，并且受制于食品生产、物流、销售和消费的各个环节。通过数据分析、市场调研和用户研究，设计师试图揭示系统不同元素之间的相关性和因果关系，提供食物浪费的整体视图。设计师批判性地思考过去和现在的生活方式，以及在未来如何重新定义人与食物之间的关系，塑造可持续的未来。

This project attempts to prove from the data analysis that food waste is a systemic problem, which is not only related to the behavior and habits of individuals, but also affected by the natural environment, historical origins, policy formulation, cultural traditions and technological development, and is subject to all aspects of food production, logistics, sales and consumption. Through data analysis, market research and user research, designers try to uncover correlations and causal relationships between different elements of the system, providing a holistic view of food waste. Designers think critically about past and present lifestyles, and how the relationship between people and food can be redefined in the future to shape a sustainable future.

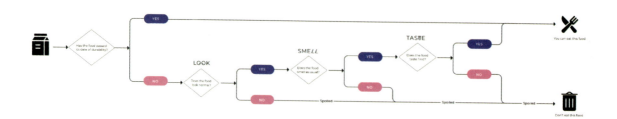

图1 食物浪费与用户行为分析

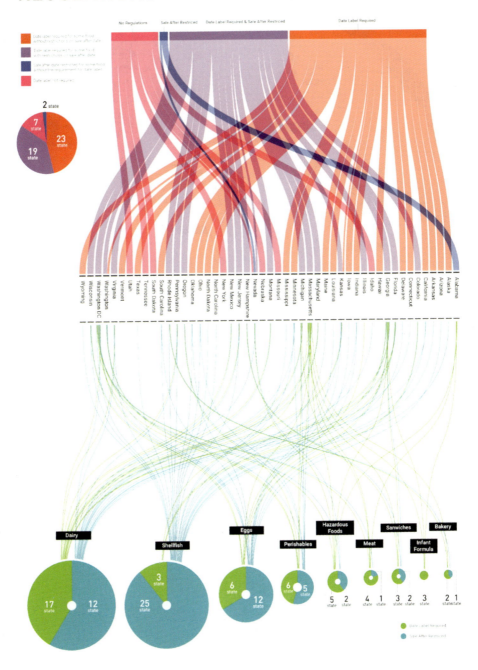

图2 美国各州食品日期标注立法比较

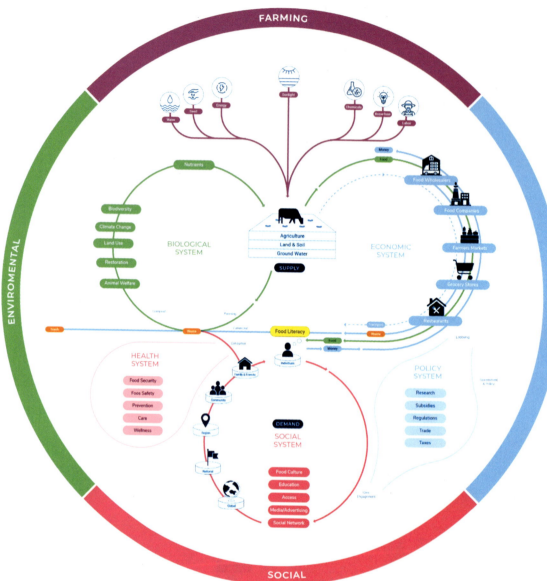

图3 食品生产与消费生态系统

Where does food waste take place?

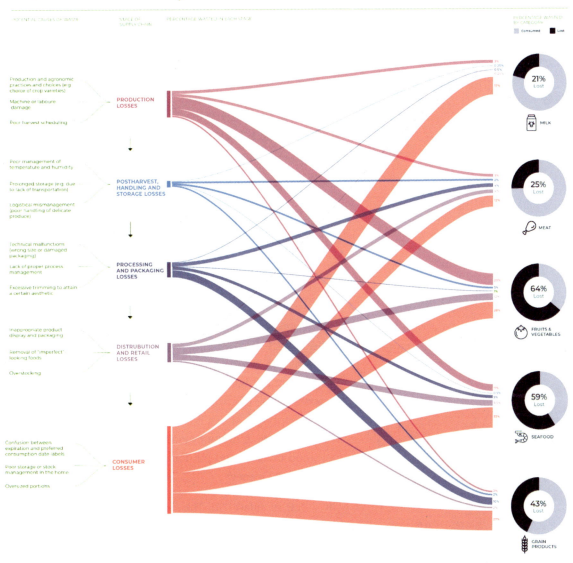

图4 食物浪费的主要区域数据可视化

121

闻香识旅人：气味图书馆品牌推广策划

TO THE FRAGRANCE: SCENT LIBRARY BRAND PROMOTION PLANNING

作者姓名
何斌 He Bin

作品形式
品牌策划
视觉设计
信息设计
Branding Planning
Visual Design
Information Design

指导教师
闵洁 Min Jie

图1 "气味图书馆"品牌形象设计应用

本设计为品牌的推广策划，即《闻香识旅人》与一系列品牌形象设计与策划。根据近年中国香水市场的调研与产品属性分析，确定了大学生市场的存在与重要性；针对品牌现存问题，重新设定品牌定位，提出"找回自我"的品牌理念。

本项目命名为《闻香识旅人》，可分"闻香"与"旅人"两部分解读。"闻"兼具"听"与"嗅"，所以"闻香"不仅用鼻子，同时也需要用心去聆听。每个人都是"旅人"，在自己生命的旅程中，我们都需要在不同的时间与空间里重新认识自我。"闻香识旅人"就是通过用心倾听、仔细体会进而认识自我，明确自己的去向，继续自己的"旅程"。个人如斯，企业如斯。

This design is the promotion planning of the brand, namely the project "To The Fragrance" and a series of brand image design and planning. According to the research and product attribute analysis of China's perfume market in recent years, the existence and importance of the college student market has been determined. Aiming at the existing problems of the brand, this design hope to reset the brand position and put forward the brand concept of "Recovering Oneself".

The book is titled "To The Fragrance", which can be divided into two parts: "Smell the Fragrance" and "The Traveler". "Smell" is "listening" and "smelling", so smell not only uses the nose, but also needs to listen with the heart. Everyone is a "traveler", and in the journey of our own life, we all need to re-understand ourselves in different time and space. "To The Fragrance" is to know oneself by listening attentively and carefully experiencing it, clarifying one's whereabouts, and continuing one's "journey". This is true for individuals, and for enterprises.

{氣味}圖書館
DEMETER
FRAGRANCE LIBRARY

氣味圖書館

我們出售的不是香水
因為香水只是一種載體
我們出售的不是回憶
因為回憶只屬於你自己
我們出售的只是氣味
在記憶裡你曾經歷過的氣味
在漫漫旅途中認識真正的你
找回已被忘卻的自我
——
聞香識旅人

气味能快速、有效地确立一个人的形象，增添其魅力。适当地使用香水，能令人神清气爽，缓解压力，周身充满活力。香水是用香料、酒精和蒸馏水等制成的化妆品。在古代，香被用于神佛祭物、净化身心，东方人最先将其使用于日常生活中。多数中国人欣赏清淡如花的香水味道，这也是亚洲人的特点。同时，香水也是送给恋人的最佳选择。

香水使用禁忌：

避免喷洒于暴露部位

避免喷洒过浓过多的香水

避免涂在易出汗的部位

避免喷洒在珠宝上

避免喷洒在白色衣物上

避免多种复方香水混合使用

避免孕妇使用香水

香水使用部位：

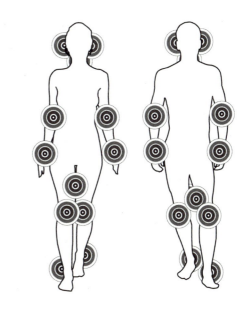

涂香的部位根据动脉的分布：耳朵后面、脖子后面、手腕内侧、大腿内侧、膝关节以及脚踝

图2　"气味图书馆"产品功效信息设计图解

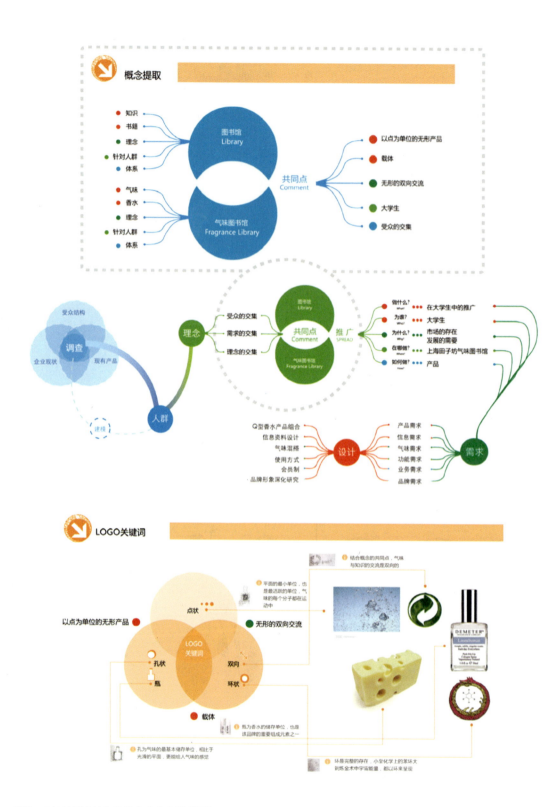

图3　"气味图书馆"品牌定位信息设计图解

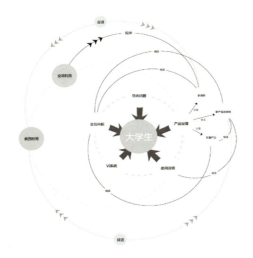

气味图书馆官方博客日志内容

加盟代理 8%
开博 4%
合作 18%
招聘 12%
YOHO网店 8%
新品发布 4%
香知识 22%
新店开幕 14%
活动宣传 10%

香水的分类：
PARTITION

香　精，赋香率约为18-25%，持续时间约7-9小时，价格昂贵且容量小。
香　水，赋香率为12-18%，持续时间3-4小时，价格比一般香水略高。
淡香水，泛指一般淡香水，赋香率约为7-12%，持续的时间2-3小时。价格最便宜，也是最常见、最被广泛使用的一种。对于第一次尝试香水的试用者是个不容易出错的选择，从居家到办公都适宜。
古龙水，赋香率大约为3-7%，持续时间约1-2小时，价格最便宜。

试香的学问：
KONWLEDGE

试香时，先将香水喷在手腕上或是试香纸上，等香水干了再闻。从开瓶到试香大约三分钟，一般香水具有三段式香味，由前味、中味、后味表现出韵律感。在试香水时，可向空中喷洒香水，再用手拨接味道至鼻边闻，此时呈现中味及后味，为香水的主调。最好不要在饥饿时去试香，如此会对香味产生恶心感。

香水的三段式：
KONWLEDGE

前味：香水喷在肌肤上约十分钟左右后会有遮盖住的香味产生。最初会有香味和挥发性高的酒精稍稍混在一起的感觉。
中味：在前味之后十分钟左右的香味，酒精味道消失，此时的香味是香水原本的味道。
后味：香水喷洒约三十分钟后才会有的香味，是表现个性最好的香味。这种香味会混合个人肌肤以及体味所产生的综合味道。

例
EXAMPLE

气味混搭

平装书 X ml

+   +

混合

霉味 X ml   灰尘 X ml

=

老式图书馆

气味图书馆小提示
NOTES

1、不管现今三调香水如何盛行，之后香水的流行趋势是单调和多调，DEMETER香水主要为单调性香水。

2、不要以留香时长来判断香水的好坏。香水的不同类型决定了留香时间，也是提供不同的选择。

3、混搭也有规则，同系列和同香系列混搭一般比较和谐，如是生手，互补类型混搭，建议谨慎调配。

4、由香水调配的先后顺序、浓淡程度不同，场景制造结果会有差异，程度的控制取决于经验和喜好。

5、气味无男女之分，只有适合与不适合。DEMETER的大多数气味为中性词，凭自己喜好与个性而定。

6、香水并不只是早晨的功课，而是像化妆品一样需要随身携带，3小时后即需要补一补。

图4　"气味图书馆"品牌定位信息设计图解

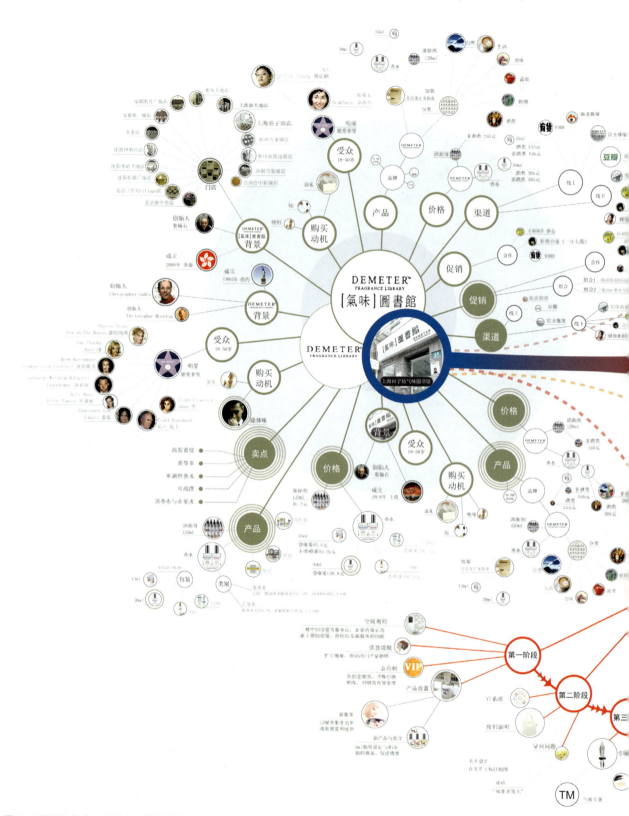

图5 "闻香识旅人"品牌主题策划信息设计图解

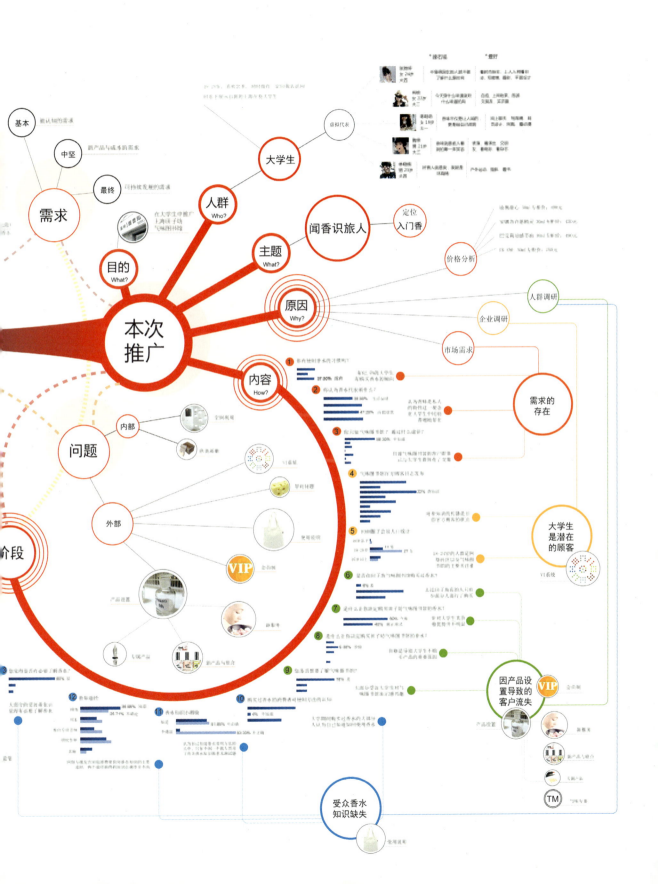

VIS基础部分
The Part of Design

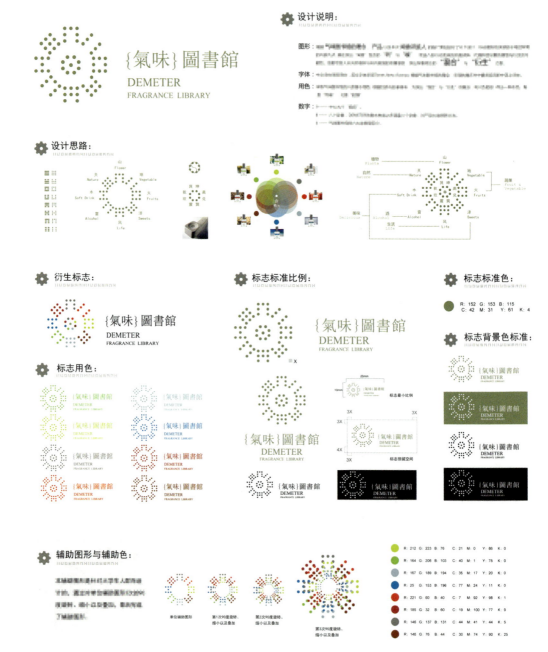

图6 "气味图书馆"品牌形象设计与应用

VIS应用部分
The Part of Prouducts

⚙ 产品包装改进设计：

氣味圖書館

我們出售的不是香水
因為香水只是一種載體
我們出售的不是回憶
因為回憶只屬於你自己
我們出售的只是 氣味
在記憶里你曾經歷過的氣味
找回已被忘卻的自我
在漫漫旅途中認識真正的你
——聞香識旅人

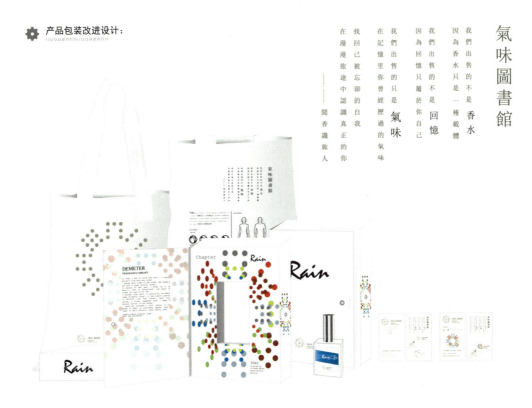

⚙ 办公类应用： **⚙ 环境类应用：**

图7 "气味图书馆"品牌形象设计与应用

有机食物网络营销应用探究
ORGANIC FOOD NETWORK STRATEGIES

作者姓名
汤雨橙　Tang Yucheng

作品形式
品牌策划
品牌设计
Branding Planning
Branding Design

指导教师
闵洁　Min Jie

今天，人们越来越注重生活的品质，传统的饮食习惯也发生了改变，健康、科学、环保的生活理念日益被大众所提倡。于是，绿色食品走进了大众生活。同时，互联网飞速发展，从网络交流、网络搜索到电子商务，已成为人们生活中必不可少的工具。

本设计从绿色产品网络营销入手，分析了当下中国绿色农产品的市场现状，以"番茄农庄"绿色食品为案例，结合当前中国网络市场以及网络消费者购买行为特征，解析企业如何运用网络营销更好地与客户沟通，从而打造良好的品牌形象，最终为企业赢得声誉与利润。

Today, people pay more and more attention to the quality of life, traditional eating habits have also changed, and the concept of healthy, scientific and environmentally friendly lifestyle is increasingly advocated by the public. As a result, green food has entered the public life. At the same time, the rapid development of the Internet, from network communication, network search to e-commerce, etc., has become an indispensable tool in people's lives.

This design starts from the online marketing of green products, and analyzes the current market situation of green agricultural products in China. Taking Tomato Farm's green food as a case, combined the current Chinese online market and the characteristics of online consumers' purchasing behavior, it analyzes how enterprises can use online marketing to better communicate with customers, so as to create a good brand image, and ultimately win the reputation and profit for the enterprise.

本次问卷以关于绿色食品的认知、渠道、服务等问题，以网络调查的方式向上海地区居民投放了120封调查问卷，回收问卷107份，有效问卷93份。受调查人群年龄段分布广，职业也各不相同，为绿色食品的研究提供了有力的数据支持。

1.您是否听说过绿色食品？

100%　总　男　女

2.您是否考虑过购买食用绿色食品？

总 75%　　男 65%　　女 85%

3.您购买绿色食品的原因是？

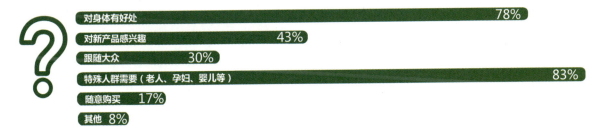

对身体有好处 78%
对新产品感兴趣 43%
跟随大众 30%
特殊人群需要（老人、孕妇、婴儿等）83%
随意购买 17%
其他 8%

4.您平常从什么渠道购买绿色食品？

超市　菜场　食品专卖店　网络

	超市	菜场	食品专卖店	网络
总	27%	43%	11%	19%
男	36%	28%	18%	18%
女	18%	58%	4%	20%

5.您是否会考虑购买绿色食品（或绿色食品消费卡）送给亲友？

GREEN FOOD

	不会	会	
总	11%	89%	
男	7%	93%	
女	15%	85%	

图1　绿色有机食物网络营销的市场调研

图2 绿色有机食物网络营销应用的信息设计图解

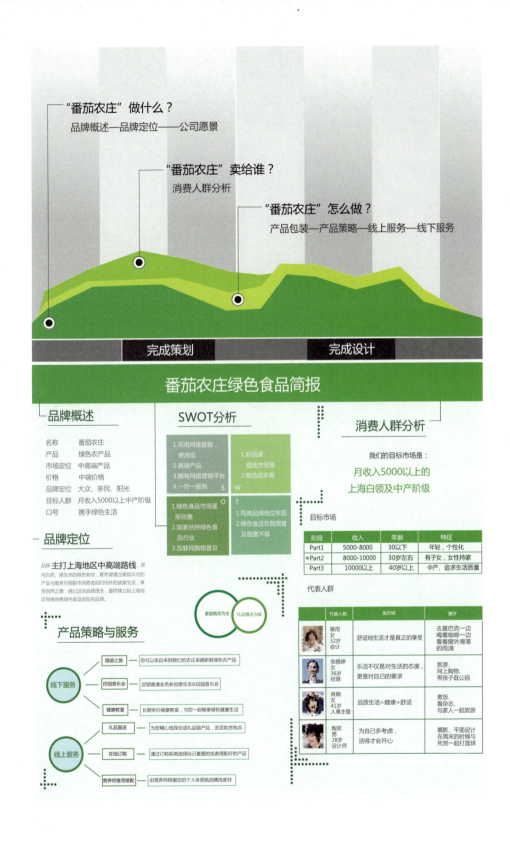

"番茄农庄"做什么？
品牌概述—品牌定位——公司愿景

"番茄农庄"卖给谁？
消费人群分析

"番茄农庄"怎么做？
产品包装—产品策略—线上服务—线下服务

完成策划　　　完成设计

番茄农庄绿色食品简报

品牌概述

名称　　　番茄农庄
产品　　　绿色农产品
市场定位　中高端产品
价格　　　中端价格
品牌定位　大众、亲民、阳光
目标人群　月收入5000以上中产阶级
口号　　　携手绿色生活

品牌定位

品牌主打上海地区中高端路线，崇尚自然、原生态的绿色食材，更希望通过番茄农庄的产品与服务引领都市消费者回归轻松的健康生活，享受自然之意，通过这些品牌理念，最终建立起上海地区网络销售绿色食品的知名品牌。

SWOT分析

1.采用网络直销，费用低
2.高端产品
3.拥有网络营销平台
4.一对一服务　S

1.新品牌，健陆市场卷
2.物流成本高　W

1.绿色食品市场逐渐完善
2.国家扶持绿色食品行业
3.互联网购物普及　O

1.同类品牌地位牢固
2.绿色食品在我国普及程度不够　T

消费人群分析

我们的目标市场是：
月收入5000以上的
上海白领及中产阶级

目标市场

阶段	收入	年龄	特征
Part1	5000-8000	30以下	年轻，个性化
*Part2	8000-10000	30岁左右	有子女，女性持家
Part3	10000以上	40岁以上	中产、追求生活质量

代表人群

代表人物	座右铭	爱好
蒋雨 女 32岁 会计	舒适地生活才是真正的享受	去星巴克一边喝着咖啡一边看着窗外滑落的雨滴
张雅婷 女 36岁 经理	乐活不仅是对生活的态度，更是对自己的要求	旅游、网上购物、带孩子逛公园
肖婉 女 41岁 人事主管	品质生活=健康+舒适	煮饭、看杂志、与家人一起旅游
陶笑 男 28岁 设计师	为自己多考虑，活得才会开心	摄影、平面设计在周末的时候与死党一起打篮球

产品策略与服务

家庭购买为主　礼品赠送为辅

线下服务
- 绿源之旅　您可以亲自来到我们的农庄采摘新鲜绿色农产品
- 田园音乐会　定期邀请会员参加原生态&田园音乐会
- 健康教室　长期举办健康教室，与您一起畅享绿色健康生活

线上服务
- 礼品直送　为您精心选择合适礼品装产品，送至收货地点
- 在线订购　通过订购系统选择自己喜欢的或者搭配好的产品
- 营养师推荐搭配　由营养师根据您的个人体质挑选精选食材

B/
05

-

产品开发类

Vitability: 健康生活方式推广品牌
VITABILITY: HEALTHY LIFESTYLE BRANDING

作者姓名
米凯尔·李 Mikael Lee

作品形式
品牌设计
包装设计
信息设计
Brand Design
Package Design
Information Design

指导教师
王琛 Chen Wang
瑟伦·摩尔 Theron Moore

图1 产品包装设计

健康的身体源于健康的生活方式：包括心理、情感和生理健康。Viability提供个性化的食品健康咨讯服务，根据用户的生活、学习和工作习惯，帮助用户生成合理均衡的膳食计划并补充需要的维生素，用个性化的方案迎合个体需求的独特性，多彩的设计风格能活跃用户的生活，为用户带来健康和充满活力的每一天。

Viability一词是Vitamin（维生素）、Vitality（活力）和Ability（能力）三个英文单词的组合，Viability健康品牌提供即时的营养健康咨讯和简洁易用的工具。Viability的目标受众是年龄在 20 至 50 岁之间的城市人群。如今，人们很难获得忙碌的生活方式所必需的营养，但Viability可以通过我们完整和均衡的营养计划填补可能存在的营养缺口。

A healthy body results from a healthy lifestyle - including mental, emotional and physical health. Viability provides personalized food health information services, according to the users' life style and work habits, to help users generate a reasonable and balanced plan for meal and vitamin supplements, and use the personalized plan to meet the uniqueness of individual needs. The colorful design styles try to activate and engage the user's daily life in a healthy and energetic way.

The word Viability is a combination of three English words, Vitamin, Vitality and Ability. The Viability health brand provides timely nutritional health information and simple and easy-to-use tools for urban people. Tailor a sound nutrition and meal plan to give them a healthy and vibrant life. The target audience is the urban population between the ages of 20 and 50. Today, it can be difficult for people to get the nutrients necessary for busy lifestyles, but Viability can fill possible nutritional gaps with our complete and balanced nutrition plan.

图2 产品品牌和健康信息设计

Colors

Primary Colors

● RGB 204/236/252
#64bc47

● RGB 66/21/11
#42150b

Secondary Colors

● RGB 66/21/11
#f15c25

● RGB 253/214/185
#fdd6b9

● RGB 72/194/197
#48c2c5

● RGB 204/236/252
#ccecfc

● RGB 227/105/126
#e3697e

● RGB 248/217/232
#f8d9e8

● RGB 182/207/63
#b6cf3f

● RGB 214/232/181
#d6e8b5

● RGB 128/44/143
#802c8f

● RGB 228/211/229
#e4d3e5

图3 产品品牌视觉设计

图4 产品品牌和健康信息设计

图5 产品品牌和健康信息设计

图6 产品包装设计

图7 产品包装设计

餐饮包装由三部分组成；主菜单、副菜单和维生素饮品。包装结构就像一个拼装玩具，三个不同形状的
盒子聚在一起合成一个六边形。此外，连接两个纸质托架的松紧带可以收紧盒子并用作包装盒的提手。

VITAMIN CONTAINER

Color Coding by Supplement Category

 Specialty Supplements   Minerals   Herbals & Botanicals   Vitamins

Daily Take Indicator

You can keep track of whether you take your vitamins with the 'Daily Take Indicator' band, on the bottom of the container. For example, if you take a vitamin in the morning, you should turn the 'Daily Take Indicator' band to show the morning icon.

Easy to Get a Tablet

Never worry about spilling tablets or counting them out. Push up the knob, on the back of the container, to release the desired number of tablets easily.

图8 产品包装设计

Water Enhancer

Color Coding by Flavors

 Raspberry & Apple   Acai & Blueberry   Lemon

Pour Water and Drink It

A water enhancer bag has a fast melting vitamin table. Tear off the top of the bag, pour water, and drink straight from the bag.

图9 产品包装设计

140

图10 产品包装设计

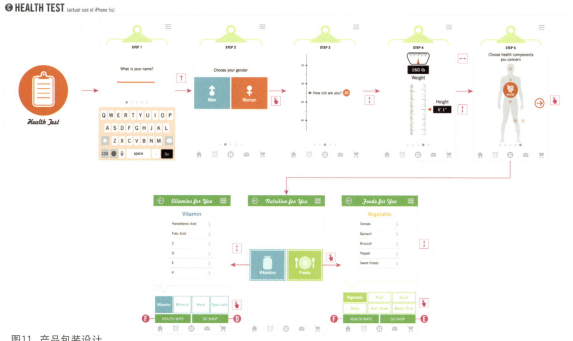

图11 产品包装设计

HAND: 智能家居管理系统设计
SMART HOME MANAGEMENT SYSTEM DESIGN

作者姓名
大卫 · 欧 David Oh

作品形式
信息设计
用户体验设计
用户界面设计
Information Design
UX/UI Design

指导教师
王琛 Chen Wang

图1 视觉标识

图2 H代表了Human（人类）

目前的智能家居设备管理机制过于复杂，没有统一的操作系统来整合不同设备之间的联系。因此，日常智能家居用户并没有享受到一套完整的家庭自动化管理系统带来的美好体验。该设计研究强调了解当前的家庭自动化系统并探索智能家居管理系统设计中存在的用户体验问题，但并不试图从工程师的角度提出具体的技术解决方案。引入的设计解决方案是对更好的用户体验设计的持续探索，以解决当今智能家居环境中的设备管理问题。

The current device management mechanisms for smart home system are too complex and do not share a unified operating system. As a result, everyday smart home users face challenges to enjoy a full home automation experience. The design research emphasizes understanding the current home automation system and exploration of the conceptual user experience design process. However, the design does not attempt to present concrete technical solutions from the engineer's point of view. The introduced design solution is an on-going search for a better user experience design to address device management in a smart home environment of today.

The Title Concept

图3 HAND 是家居智能管理系统的品牌名称，设计用人手作为视觉元素来表达交互和沟通的含义，同时，四个英文组成字母分别是Human（人类）、AI（人工智能）、Network（网络）和Device（设备）四个单词的首写字母

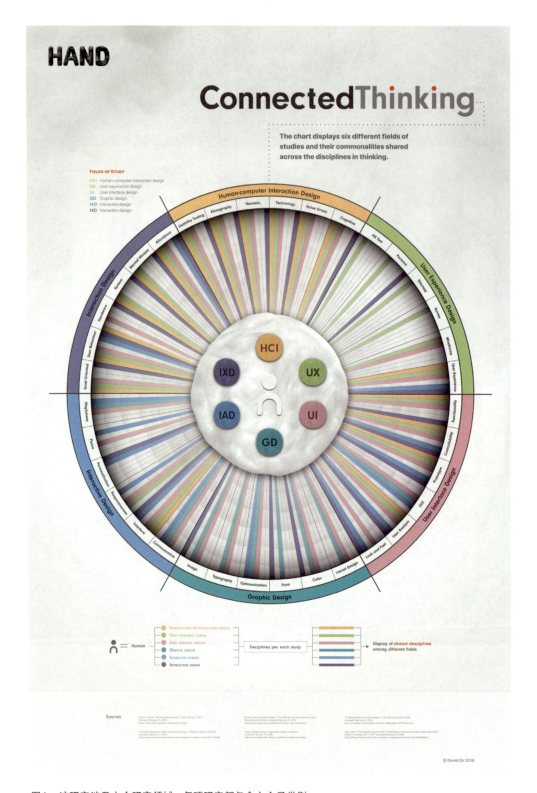

图4 该研究涉及六个研究领域，每项研究都包含六个子类别

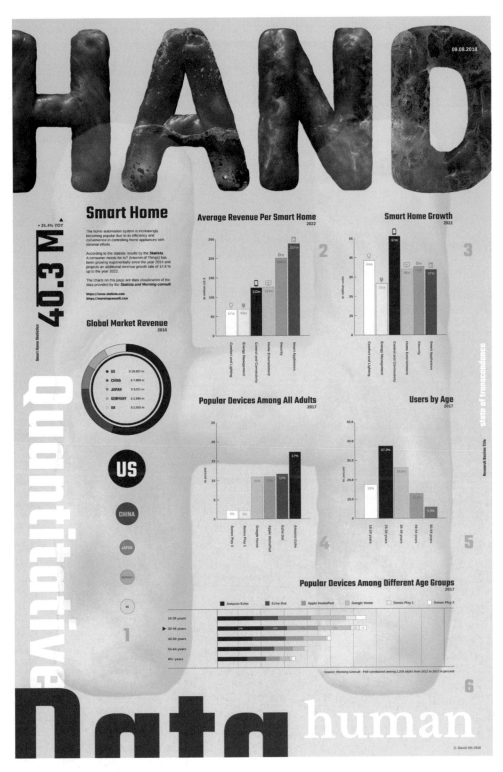

图5　市场量化数据的分析

Smart Home Automation

INITIATION

User activates smart home system
with all human senses.

- AI wall screen with data analysis and feedback
- Universal set of gestures | Customizable options
- User pattern | behaviour prediction
- Conversational voice command
- Tutorial App to sync with AI
- Mixture of voice, gesture, and touch to initiate

CONTROL

User interacts with AI system
that controls all devices.

- Centralized AI home system communicates with
  both users and devices
- Master admin
- 3D projections | All sides wall screens
- Informative notifications and alerts
- Machine learning
- Automatic setting allows AI to adjust devices by itself

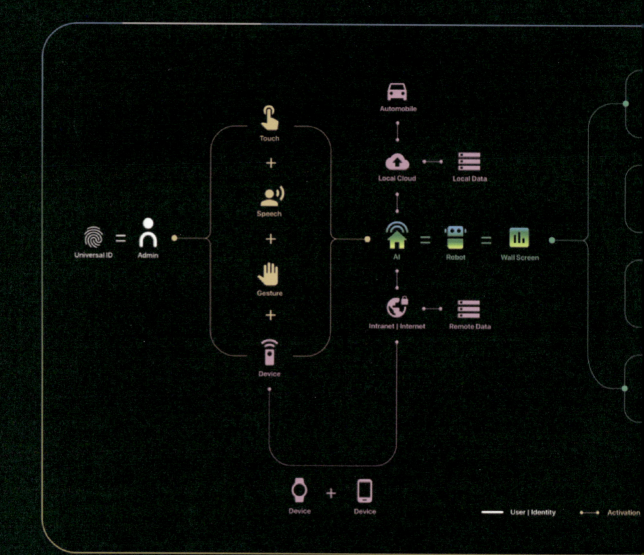

MAP

■ MANAGEMENT

User can manage AI and all devices
by using an universal App.

- Universal ID
- Biometric authentication including heartbeat
- AI voice summary and suggestions
- Automatic call during medical emergency
- App is the AI
- Local cloud as well as remote cloud

■ REMOTE ACCESS

User can directly contact AI
to remotely access all devices.

- Sync with an automobile
- Temp ID for guest
- Robotic AI assistant
- Communicate directly to AI from anywhere
- Built in interface system throughout the house
- Renewable energy cycles in between rooms

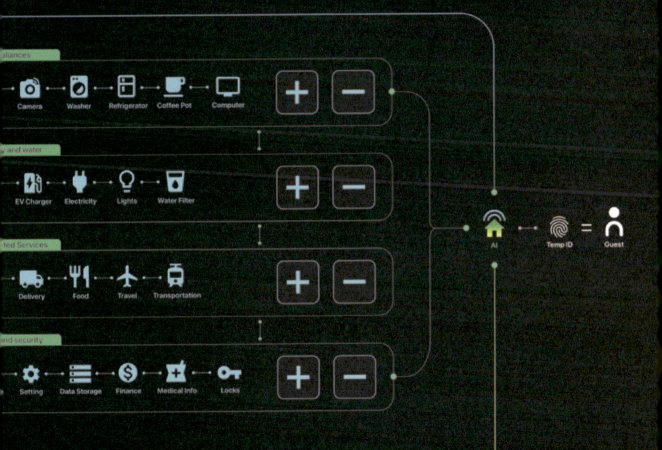

图6　智能家居生态系统概述图

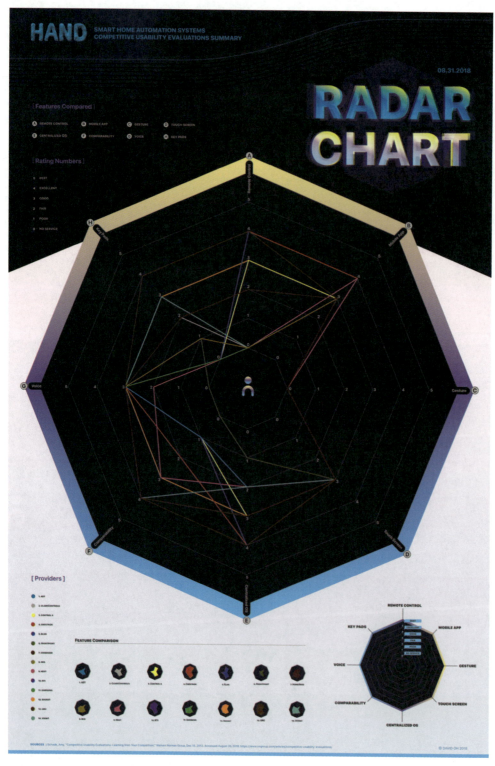

图7　市场产品竞争性评估总结图

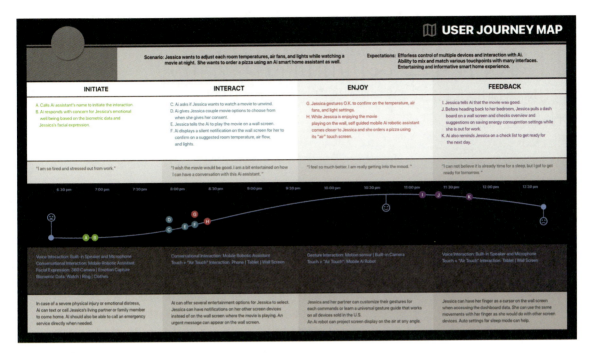

图8 用户流程图

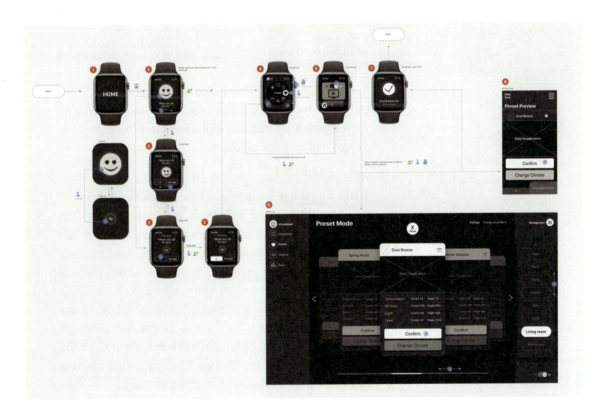

图9 用户的工作场景与流程图

149

方寸: 家居园艺装饰品牌市场推广

FANG CUN: MARKETING OF HOUSEHOLD GARDEN ADORNMENT BRAND

作者姓名
程小雨 Cheng Xiaoyu

作品形式
品牌策划
产品设计
Branding Planning
Product Design

指导教师
闵洁 Min Jie

图1 "方寸" 家居园艺装饰品牌产品设计

互联网时代, 人们接触绿色的时间越来越少。这款设计产品让人们在室内能够拥有属于自己的一隅绿色休闲之地。方寸是形容空间面积大小的词汇, 用以作为创意花盆容器的品牌名。其核心理念为: 简单种植, 乐趣拼接。

在进行针对各类花盆容器的市场调研后, 发现国内市场上缺少创意花盆, 由此, "方寸" 系列产品应运而生。这是一款既能摆放在桌面又能悬挂于墙上的植物容器。灵感来源于乐高的拼接原理, 由底板和花盆两部分组成, 购买者可以有各种不同造型、风格、颜色的产品选择, 同时根据室内空间的大小定制植物与花盆。"方寸" 期望能在人们享受室内种植的同时带来拼接的乐趣。

In the Internet era, people are less and less exposed to green plants. This design solution allows people to have their own corner of green retreated indoors. Fang Cun, a term that describes the size of a small space, is used as a creative brand name of pot containers. Its core idea: simple planting, fun stitching.

After market research on various types of pot containers, it was found that there was a lack of creative pots in the domestic market, and as a result, the series of Fang Cun products came into being. It is a plant container that can be placed on the table and hung on the wall. Inspired by Lego's stitching principle, it consists of two parts: a baseplate and a flower pot, and buyers can choose from a variety of different shapes, styles, and colors. At the same time, according to the size of the indoor space, the plants and pots can be customized. Fang Cun, the design solution, expect people to enjoy indoor planting which bring the pleasure of stitching to them.

图2 "方寸"家居园艺装饰品牌产品设计

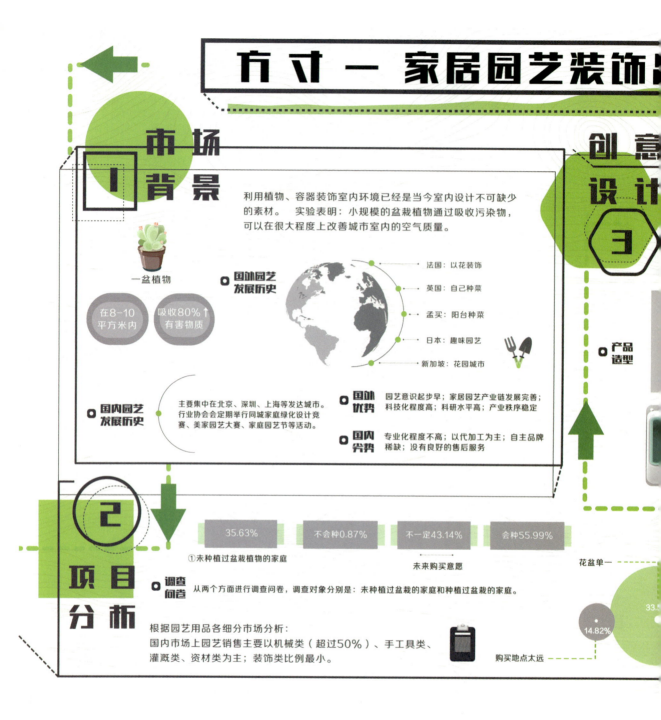

方寸 — 家居园艺装饰

市场背景 1

利用植物、容器装饰室内环境已经是当今室内设计不可缺少的素材。 实验表明：小规模的盆栽植物通过吸收污染物，可以在很大程度上改善城市室内的空气质量。

一盆植物

在8-10平方米内

吸收80%↑有害物质

国外园艺发展历史

- 法国：以花装饰
- 英国：自己种菜
- 孟买：阳台种菜
- 日本：趣味园艺
- 新加坡：花园城市

国内园艺发展历史 主要集中在北京、深圳、上海等发达城市。行业协会会定期举行同城家庭绿化设计竞赛、美家园艺大赛、家庭园艺节等活动。

国外优势 园艺意识起步早；家居园艺产业链发展完善；科技化程度高；科研水平高；产业秩序稳定

国内劣势 专业化程度不高；以代加工为主；自主品牌稀缺；没有良好的售后服务

创意设计 3

产品造型

项目分析 2

35.63%　不会种0.87%　不一定43.14%　会种55.99%

①未种植过盆栽植物的家庭　　未来购买意愿

调查问卷 从两个方面进行调查问卷，调查对象分别是：未种植过盆栽的家庭和种植过盆栽的家庭。

根据园艺用品各细分市场分析：国内市场上园艺销售主要以机械类（超过50%）、手工具类、灌溉类、资材类为主；装饰类比例最小。

花盆单一

14.82%　33.

购买地点太远

图3　"方寸"家居园艺装饰品牌市场推广信息设计图解

牌的建立及市场推广

○ 标志
设计

○ 核心
理念

简单拼接
乐趣生活

方寸
家居园艺装饰

○ 创意
来源

希望打造一款既能摆放于桌面
又能装饰在墙上的花盆容器
在解决浇水、垂直受力等问题的同时
也能兼顾美观

宣传片　微信公众号　话题讨论圈

关键词：简单种植 乐趣生活
　　　　一盆两用 随心所欲

广告语：不必担心大小
　　　　即使蜗居 也值得拥有

 线上关注公众号报名
线下参与交流会
交流会

**线上
线下
结合** ○

主办方提供花盆容器
同城举办植物（举例：多肉）交流会
邀请多肉植物达人参与交流

 利用底板，拼接图案
上传照片，为你点赞

64.37%
②种植过盆栽植物的家庭

植物不易运输

种植困难

22.48%

29.16%

室内空间太小

**私人
定制** ○

根据室内面积大小以及个人喜好
私人定制方寸的尺寸大小、颜色以及纹理

**市场
推广**

4

153

C/

对话创新设计师

-

胡安 · 曼努埃尔 · 埃斯卡兰特

约翰 · T.德鲁

庄稼昀

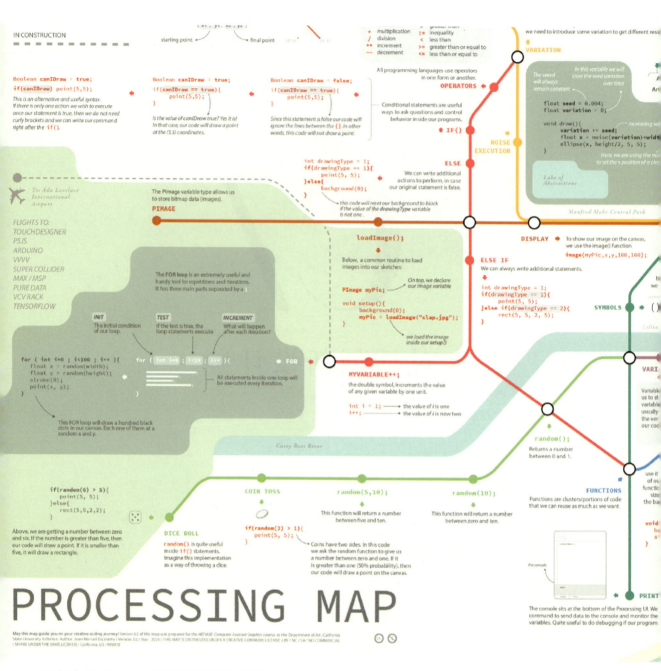

PROCESSING MAP

图形设计语言（Processing）知识节点地图 (2008–2021)

JUAN MANUEL ESCALANTE
胡安·曼努埃尔·埃斯卡兰特

KEYWORDS:

Interdisciplinary | Generative design |Interaction of virtual and reality
交叉学科，生成设计，虚拟与现实的互动

1：加州大学圣塔芭芭拉分校（UCSB）的媒体艺术与技术专业是美国首批提供艺术与科学跨界学位的学科之一，被认为是全球互动数字媒体专业的蓝本。它以运用计算思维作为创意表达手段而闻名。作为一个从那里毕业的博士生，它是否符合您的个人目标？又给您的设计实践和研究带来了哪些变化？

在墨西哥国立大学(UNAM)的建筑学研究生课程中进行了八年的研究和教学后，我开始在加州大学圣塔巴巴拉分校研读博士学位。MAT课程给了我成长为设计师和艺术家所需的空间和自由。MAT的优势之一就是拥有在众多主题上进行工作的跨学科教师，可以实践从粒子合成、系统论、触觉理论和其他形式的计算性表达。

我的视听作品在圣塔芭芭拉得以成熟，我使用当代乐器深入研究图形乐谱的分枝领域。我也在这里遇到了很棒的同事，他们中的许多人现在还在与我合作。那是充满挑战和美好的岁月，我感谢 MAT 为我的探索与研究提供的所有资源和指导。

2：生成设计如何影响内容创建、形式呈现、交互和决策的思维方式？

任何生成方法的核心都是算法，即一组完成特定任务的指令。这是一个需要大量抽象的过程。我们正在设计具有不同复杂程度的计算系统。对我有影响的人之一是贾里德·塔贝尔，他将绘画程序视为活的有机体。今天，我们不能忘记计算机模型和模拟在科学研究中的重要性。

我们可以在艺术和设计中生成这些系统，并将该领域推向新的未探索方向。在这样的情况下，可视化结果来自编程级别的抽象性。每个创造者必须决定系统如何控制五花八门的变量，如随机性、自我生成、交互、时间。计算程序可能会崩溃并产生漂亮的、意想不到的结果。作为创作者，我们必须培养知道何时纠正这些错误或拥抱混乱的敏感性。

3：人工智能和云计算将给信息设计和品牌设计领域带来哪些变化？

在过去的几十年里，我们的物种已经将大量数据数字化。每天，我们的数字交互都会贡献和扩大这些数据集。人工智能将揭示数据中的模式并发现我们可能会错过的东西，例如它在医疗领域的巨大潜力，但如果我们在全球范围内建立起大规模监控网络，也会令人担忧。我基于浏览器的项目 The Post-Surveillance Alternative Atlas (P.S.A.A.) （图1）以富有诗意的方式解决了其中一些问题。在人工智能领域，伦理问题是迫切需要解决的。我密切关注我的同事法比安·奥弗特的工作，他在计算偏置和关键的机器视觉领域拥有深刻见解。

我们面临着在视听领域解析、显示和理解此类数据的新挑战，换句话说，这是一个新的界面。如果我们了解这些系统的结构，我们将会更好地做出反应，并主动与我们的时代精神互动。对于在 UI/UX 领域工作的设计师来说，这可能是改变方向、纠正并解决当前界面所产生的社会和文化影响的理想时机。我们必须超越人工智能的现成可视化实现，在可见的层面上进行超越，并尽早将这些技术手段融入我们的工作流程之中。

4：您的一些设计作品与音乐活动和品牌有关。您能谈谈您在使用计算方法传达品牌信息方面的经验吗？

我感兴趣的是视觉组件如何以不同的方式增强听觉体验。图形乐谱是实现这一目标的一种方式。在表演环境中，我向观众展示了该系统是如何工作的。从这个角度来看，我的图表式陈述可以被看作是高度抽象化后的界面（图2）。

我们现在已不复存在的工作室Realität受委托为墨西哥城 Vive Latino音乐节的Gozadero舞台做视觉叙事。我们创建了一个符号字母表，它会一步步慢慢地向观众展示（图3）。我们为每个音乐家的表演制作了声音反应图形，并根据我们正在听的音乐匹配其强度。

尽管在Gozadero上有各种类型的表演，但我们的图表投影装置和动态图形设计为舞台带来了一种标识和凝聚力。音乐节结束后我们将图形印制成微型版发放给团队（图4）。

5：设计学科该如何应对交叉学科合作的趋势？年轻设计师需要培养和强化什么技能？

快速浏览一下当今的学术就业市场，就会发现许多职位都强调跨学科。在艺术领域，前卫艺术的一个重要方面就是将艺术、科学和技术以各种形式融为一体，这不足为奇。

将其他学科纳入其中，可以发现新的创造性探索途径。2014年，我完成了声音消化系统项目（图5）。这是一次视听探索，灵感来自我们的消化系统的机制。这个项目在一次科学会议上发表，还获得了电声作曲奖。然而，我相信我们的视听形式也可以在其他领域带来令人兴奋的发现。数据可视化是实现这一目标的一种方式，但不是唯一的方式。

今天，年轻的设计师们生活在一个奇妙的世界里，他们掌握着大量的知识和信息。但另一方面，过度曝光和饱和状态削弱了我们这一代人的专注力。这是学术界提供空间和有价值指导的地方。

6：您将创造性的编程带入课堂的情况怎样？你希望给设计领域带来哪些改变？

我是经历了没有互联网世界的一代。我的第一台电脑是Commodore 64。我必须编写一些命令才能玩电子游戏。之后，电脑变得更容易接触，网络诞生了。这是一个充满希望的时代。我们需要知道如何编写一个HTML网页或一个简短的javascript代码才能积极参与。在计算机和网络的最初几十年里，人们普遍感到很兴奋。

现在情况有些不同，数字化的东西变得无处不在。由于当今技术的某些方面发生了险恶的转变，因此编程不仅是一种理解世界的方式，也是一种抵抗的方式。编码使设计师能够在我们这个时代的围墙花园之外创造新的空间，并创建新的社区和定制工具。

让我们回到之前关于编程和设计算法的问题。我相信创作者在编写这些代码抽象概念时可以找到他们自己的声音。对我而言，编程是一种实现直觉的方式，我试图在课堂上传达这一点。代码对于初学者来说无疑是具有挑战性的。为此，我设计了一个地铁地图形式的Processing语言图（图6）。2008年以来，我在工作坊里发放了这张地图的不同版本。在图片中，每条地铁线代表每周的一个主题。地图上还有一些伪装成地标的隐藏宝石，例如Ruth Leavitt城市花园或Manfred Mohr中央公园。（图7）（图8）

在课堂教学中，编程是一个需要好奇心、实验精神、勇敢和毅力的心理过程。作为一名教育工作者，我的职责是尽可能创造更多的空间，让这些特质能够在课堂上得以发挥和拓展。

除了对创作过程的技术贡献之外，编程曾经被忽视的声音在世界范围内正在逐渐被大家认可。亲眼目睹各种各样的社区使用技术、构建自己的工具并由此更新传统的工作流程，这非常令人鼓舞！非常希望我们继续沿着这条路走下去。

1. UCSB's Media Arts and Technology (MAT) is among the first interdisciplinary graduate programs in the United States to offer a science degree in Art. It is well known for the methods of Computing Design as Meaning Making approach. As a Ph.D. graduated from there, is it a good fit with your personal goal? What changes has it brought to your design practice and research?

After eight years of research and teaching at the graduate program in Architecture at Mexico's National University (UNAM), I started my Ph.D. at UC Santa Barbara. The MAT program provided me with the space and freedom I needed to grow as a designer and artist. One of the program's strengths is its multidisciplinary faculty working in a wide range of topics, from granular synthesis to systemics, haptics, and other forms of expressive computation.

My audiovisual work matured in Santa Barbara, and I delved deeply into the subfield of graphic notation using contemporary instruments. I met fantastic colleagues, too, many of whom I still collaborate with. Those were challenging and wonderful years, and I am grateful for all the resources and guidance MAT contributed to my exploration and creative research.

2: How does generative design affect the way of thinking about content creation, form presentation, interaction, and decision-making?

At the core of any generative approach is an algorithm, a set of instructions to complete a specific task. It is a process that requires a lot of abstraction. We are designing computational systems with various degrees of complexity. One of my early influences, Jared Tarbell, approached his drawing programs as living organisms. Today, let's not forget the critical importance of computer models and simulations in scientific research.

We can generate those systems in art and design and keep pushing the field into new unexplored directions.

In such scenarios, the visual result results from an abstraction at the programming level. Each creator must decide how the system will control myriad variables such as randomness, self-generation, inter-action, time. Computer programs might break and generate beautiful, unexpected results. As creators, we must develop the sensibility to know when to correct those mistakes or embrace chaos.

3: What changes will artificial intelligence (A.I.) and cloud computing bring to the field of information design and brand design?

Our species has digitized vast amounts of data during the last few decades. Every day, our digital interactions contribute and enlarge these datasets. A.I. comes to reveal patterns in that data and discover things that we probably would have missed. The potential is enormous in the medical field, for exam-ple, but also concerning if we consider the massive surveillance networks currently in place worldwide. My browser-based project, The Post-Surveillance Alternative Atlas (P.S.A.A.)(1), addressed some of these concerns in a poetic way. Ethics in A.I. is a much-needed field today. I follow closely the work of my colleague Fabian Offert and his insightful perspective in the field of bias and critical machine vision.

We are presented with new challenges to parse, display, and understand such data in the audio-visual realm. In other words, new interfaces. If we understand how these systems are structured, we will respond better and actively engage with our zeitgeist. For designers working in the UI/UX field, this might be an ideal moment to change course, correct, and address the social and cultural impact created by our current interfaces.

We must go beyond ready-made visual implemen-tations of A.I., transcend the visible layer, and insert these techniques much earlier into our workflows.

4: Some of your design works are related to music events and brands. Can you talk about your expe-rience in using computing methods to convey branding message?

I am interested in how the visual component can enhance the listening experience in different ways. Graphic notation is one way to achieve that. In a performance setting, I offer the audience a glimpse of how the system works. From this perspective, my diagrammatic representations could be seen as highly abstracted interfaces (2).

In 2014, our now-extinct studio Realität, was commissioned to do the visual narrative for the Gozadero stage at the Vive Latino festival in Mexico City. We created an alphabet of symbols that we would slowly reveal to the audience (3). We performed our sound-reactive graphics for each musician's act and matched its intensity based on the music we were listening. Despite the various genres performed at Gozadero, our diagrammatic projections and motion design brought a sense of identity and cohesiveness to the stage. All the graphics were part of a small print edition that we distributed among our team after the festival was over. (4)

With the democratization of technology, we have seen the emergence of a new type of creator capable of composing both sounds and visuals simultane-ously. It is an exciting field to explore.

5: How does the school design discipline respond to this trend of Interdisciplinary collaboration? What kind of skills do young designers need to cultivate and strengthen?

A quick look at the academic job market today shows a multidisciplinary emphasis in many positions. In the arts, it comes as no surprise that an important part of the avant-garde blends art, science, and technology in various forms.

Bringing other disciplines into the mix can reveal new creative avenues to explore. In 2014, I completed the Sound Digestive System project(5). It was an audiovisual exploration inspired by the mechanisms of our digestive system. The project was featured in a scientific conference and won an award for electroacoustic composition. However, the process should go beyond inspiration. I believe our audiovisual forms can also lead to exciting discoveries in other fields. Data Visualization is one way of doing this, but not the only one.

Young designers live in a fantastic world today with so much knowledge and information at their disposal. On the other hand, overexposure and saturation have diminished our generation's ability to focus. This is where academia can provide space and valuable guidance.

6: You have brought creative coding into classroom setting? How was it? What changes do you expect to bring to the design field?

I come from a generation that experienced the world without the internet. My first computer was a Commodore 64. I had to write a few commands to play video games. Afterward, computers became more accessible, and the web was born. It was a hopeful time. We needed to know how to code an HTML webpage or a short javaScript code to be actively involved. There was a general excitement around the early decades of computers and the web.

Things are a bit different now; everything digital has become ubiquitous. Since some aspects of technology have taken a sinister twist these days, coding is not only a way of understanding the world but a form of résistance. Coding empowers designers to create new spaces beyond the walled gardens of our era and create new communities and customized tools.

We go back to our early conversation about programming and designing algorithmic systems. I believe creators can find their voices when writing these code abstractions. Programming for me has been a way of materializing intuition, and I try to convey that in the classroom. Code can undoubtedly be challenging for beginners. For this reason, I designed a diagram of the Processing language in the form of a subway map(6). I have distributed different versions of this map in my workshops since 2008. In the image, each subway line represents a weekly topic. The map also has a few hidden gems disguised as landmarks, such as the Ruth Leavitt City Gardens or the Manfred Mohr Central Park. (7)(8)

Inside the classroom, coding is a mental process that thrives with curiosity, experimentation, and brave perseverance. As an educator, It is my duty to create as much space as possible for such attributes to expand and develop.

Beyond the technological contribution of coding to the creative process, we are also living in a time where overlooked voices are starting to get recognized worldwide. It has been inspiring to witness a diverse range of communities approaching technology, building their own tools, and refreshing traditional workflows as a consequence. I certainly hope we continue through that path.

图1 The "Post-Surveillance Alternative Atlas" (P.S.A.A.), screen capture. (2019)

图2 The "Generation of Maps", rehearsal photograph (2020)

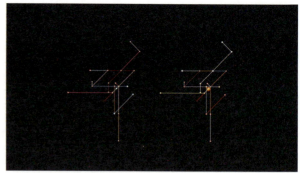

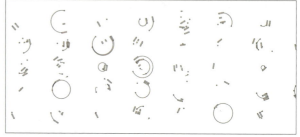

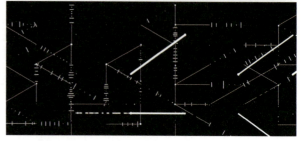

图3 "Algorithmic Works" for the Vive Latino Festival (2014)

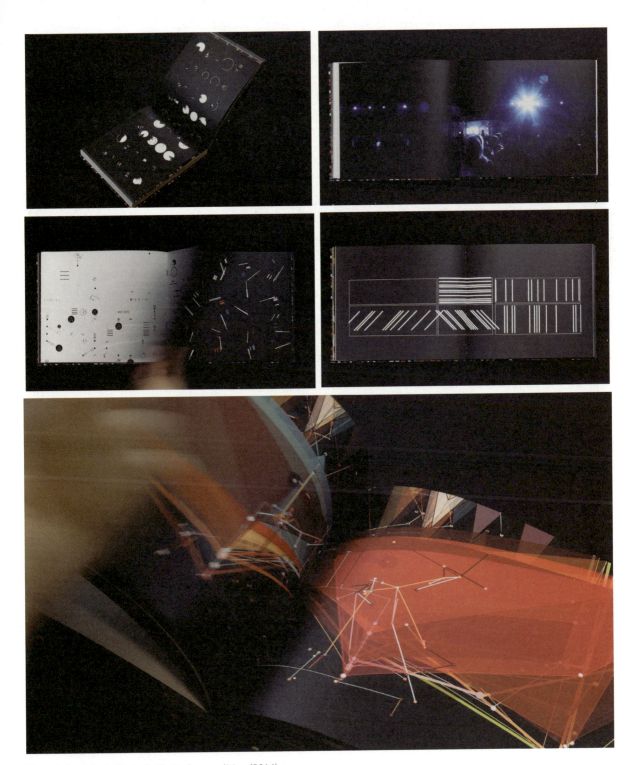

图4 "Algorithmic Works", limited-run edition (2014)

图5 "The Sound Digestive System", screen capture (2014)

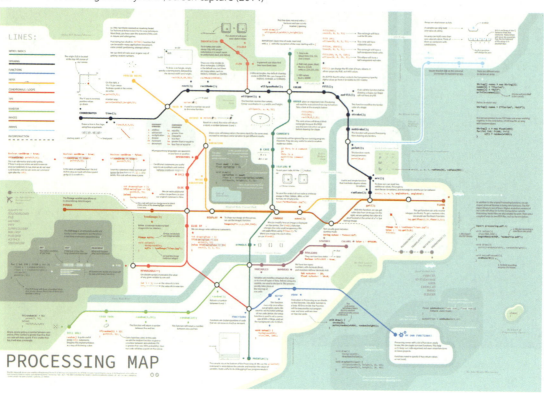

图6 "Processing Subway map" (2008–2021)

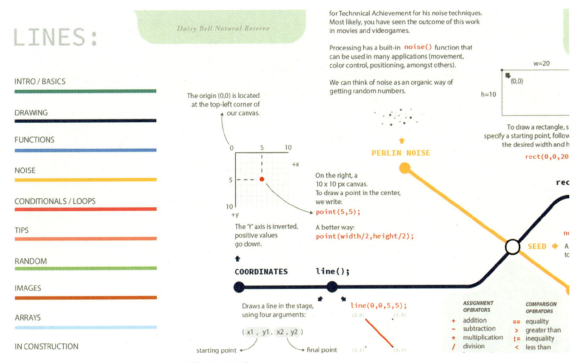

图7 "Processing Subway map", detail (2008–2021)

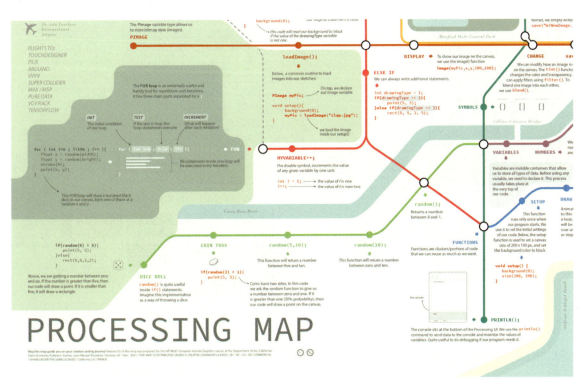

图8 "Processing Subway map", detail (2008–2021)

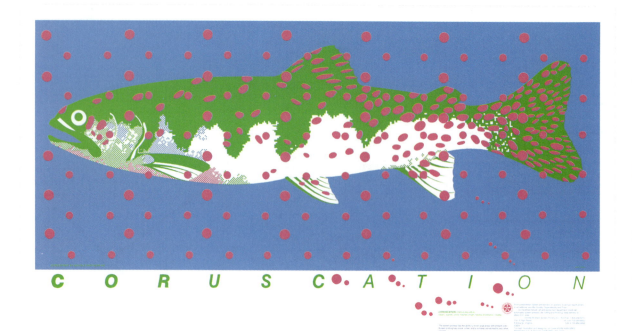

《色彩管理：色彩设计的统筹与应用》

166

JOHN T. DREW
约翰·T. 德鲁

KEYWORDS:

Design community, Accessibility and design innovation
社区文化, 无障碍设计与创新

1: 您最近发表了一篇关于无障碍设计的白皮书。您能否谈谈它的意图是什么？您预计它将给设计界带来什么变化？

这篇论文的标题是"卓越设计创新中心：APP应用程序视觉无障碍白皮书"，由莎拉·迈耶教授、热内·本尼森和我共同撰写。在白皮书中，ICDE建议个人、教育协会、高校、社会组织和企业采用新的技术标准开发应用工具，减少信息访问时的障碍。为此，本白皮书列出了一些应用工具和方法所需的资讯，目的不仅仅是为了推广新技术，同时也要求制定新的教育规范，并将这些方法、过程和原则传授给他人。白皮书所包含的信息可能帮助到全球14.9亿有信息访问障碍的人，ICDE希望这些信息不仅会成为新技术的驱动力，还能推动设计标准、立法、软件、字体以及 UI/UX 工具包、设计模板等的更新。

我们现在可以科学地检测距离、印刷方式、颜色和动态对视力的影响，包括 20/20 视力标准和其他视力标准下的盲人和视力障碍者。书中包含的信息还包括颜色、亮度值、Y三色值、颜色对比度及如何测量它们；字体、用于最大化观看距离的字形结构、用于计算不同视力的观看距离的测量值、字体观看距离表以及如何最好地设计它，以便于给有视力障碍的人提供有用的科学资讯。信息无障碍（Accessibility）是ICDE免费教育项目的核心。ICDE认为，创建一个无障碍、所有人都可以访问的教育信息环境（无论其残障程度如何），是可以实现的，也是有必要的。

2: 无障碍设计标准是专门为残障人士制定的？还是基于以人为本的设计理念制定的更为广泛的实践指导？

无障碍设计是以人为本设计（HCD）的子集，不应该和通用设计相混淆，通用设计本身就是一个子集。通用设计的原则是创建所有人都可访问的对象或环境，例如，人行道坡道或可以为任何人打开的自动门。无障碍设计专门针对不同类型的残障人士，并为一系列满足残障人士需求的产品（例如 iPhone 应用程序）创建/开发新工具、标准、原则和最佳设计实践。

最终，如果开发的产品对所有用户都有用，那它可以被归类为通用设计，但它已经融入了针对目标用户的设计实践。而HCD则使用一种将用户放在首位的方法，通过研究最终用户来培养同理心。正如热内·本尼森教授所解释的："为了创造价值，产品的功能必须以四种不同的方式满足人们的需求。[1]

1. 产品必须帮助或支持用户想要达到的目标。

2. 功能必须是可靠的，人们才会相信它的目的。

3. 产品的功能必须在各种情况下都能使用。

4. 要创造价值，产品的运行也必须是令人愉悦的。[2]

如果用户的需求没有在这四个方面都得到满足，产品的价值就无法发挥其潜力，用户也不会觉得产品有意义。"

HCD 的方式当然可以用来帮助解决可访问性的设计问题或者通用设计问题。事实上，HCD 和改善可访问性问题的设计工具和原则经常被一起使用，以便在使用方法和物理需求上达成一致性，并在这一系列的反馈循环中形成设计和产品。

3： 你能列出无障碍设计标准的一些基本原则吗？

首先，世界各地的视觉传达设计教育必须教授三维色彩理论。其他设计学科，比如产品设计、材料设计、建筑和室内建筑等都应该了解并使用它。三维色彩理论由光源（加色理论）、物体（减色理论）和观察者组成。而这三个部分正是我们教育过程中缺失的。目前的情况是，观察者是坐在电脑前的设计师，他们不知道如何为有障碍的人进行设计，他们也不了解这三者（光源、对象和观察者）有何不同的情境、它们该如何匹配、以及如何协同工作来解决问题。

三维色彩理论使用不同类型的色彩测量方法，例如，照度值和三色值两者都用来衡量人类对颜色的反应。在网页设计中，照度值用来测量颜色对比度，并且有许多网站（请参见下面的链接[3]）测量并确定涉及的色调是否具有足够的颜色对比度以满足视障（20/70）人群。美国残疾人法案（ADA）和万维网联盟（WC3）定义了视障人士的色彩对比度。

为了确保（类型、图标、徽标或符号）对象在一定距离外能被看到，物体最薄的部分必须以点为单位测量。黑白单点线对应 20/20 视力的观察距离为 5 英尺，对应 20/70 视力的观察距离为 1.455 英尺。换句话说，对应 20/20 视力，白色背景上的黄橙色单点线的观察距离只有1英尺，损失了80%。而相同场景下，20/70 的观察距离是0.311英尺，大约只有4 英寸。所以设计师尝试为视障人士设计是不可能的，因为他们没有接受过这样的培训。

为视障人士创建照片时，对象之间的颜色对比度必须达到40 CVD。若要确定照片中的对象是否具有所需的颜色对比度，要使用经典数字色表来测量对象、对象和背景(任何边缘与另一边缘接触的地方)。换句话说，在拍摄照片之前，需要了解物体和背景之间所需的对比度。在拍摄前，必须始终考虑如何在镜头中定位对象。在拍摄之前决定颜色比在拍摄后处理照片要容易得多。对于视障人士来说，摄影极简主义是最好的方法。

最后，需要了解您正在创建的设计的目标距离。例如，iPhone、iPad、杂志和书籍的阅读距离都在18到24英寸之间。笔记本电脑的工作距离为 30 英寸，台式电脑的工作距离为 33 到 36 英寸。

4： 从设计策略的角度来看，信息设计和创新的关系是什么？或者说信息设计如何引导品牌创新？

爱德华·塔夫特说得最好："杂乱和混乱是设计的失败，而不是信息的属性。"如果设计师拥有准确的信息，那其必将产生更好的解决方案。当你对主题理解越深，就越能发挥洞察力和创新力。设计师利用天赋从他们的想象中创造品牌的时代已经结束了。事实上，我觉得这些日子从未存在过。信息设计及其方法、过程和实践有助于直观地构建研究框架，使其易于被用户和客户理解。信息设计是理解

1   Walter, Aarron. *Designing for Emotion*. A Book Apart/
Jeffrey Zeldman, 2011.

2   Walter, Aarron. *Designing for Emotion*. A Book Apart/
Jeffrey Zeldman, 2011.

3   https://toolness.github.io/accessible-color-matrix
https://www.easyrgb.com/en/convert.php
https://www.icde.co

复杂信息并揭示模式、特征和事实以确定方法的逻辑方法。信息设计也可以是一种解决方案。换句话说，创新来自于识别组成品牌的复杂网络和相互关联的系统，如果做得好，信息设计会在一个易于理解的框架中衍生出品牌生态系统。

5：你个人研究的另一个重点是创新设计，包括建立一个非营利的创意社区。它的目标是什么？如何能提升设计社区的创造力？

ICDE[4] 是一家非营利组织，致力于为贫困的设计学生提供教育机会。ICDE 将与我们的企业赞助商（包括该领域的专业人士）合作，为这些学生提供奖学金、实习和指导计划。"根据美国人口普查报告，2015年25岁及以上的美国人口中只有32.5%拥有学士学位，只有12% 拥有高级学位（专业、硕士、或博士学位）"。这根本不够。很多有才华的人都被抛在了后面。ICDE 相信，世界上的许多问题都可以通过教育和机会来解决。ICDE 认为，创建所有人都可以接收的教育环境，无论这些人是否残疾，是可以实现且必要的，通过我们的免费教育资源，我们培训学生成为无障碍设计师。通过我们的网站，ICDE 提供免费的教育资源给任何在平面或传播设计领域有热情和需求的人。这些教育资源通过文章、讲座、教程、链接和帖子不断更新，内容由董事会成员、大使和该领域内的教育工作者审核，涵盖设计中的20多个学科或子学科。此外，ICDE 还赞助全国学生设计竞赛，以帮助这些学生在该领域获得认可。目前，ICDE 举办了10多场全国性比赛，并计划举办更多比赛。卓越设计创新中心的愿景是成为变革的推动者，并为对设计充满热情和需求的个人提供改变生活的机会。

ICDE 具有独特的优势，可以充分利用设计行业、教育界、各个领域不同的公司、商业伙伴、年轻人才和那些对设计具有热情和需求的个人的专业知识，是将这些不同的领域人才聚集在一起的地方。我们提供创造机会、分享想法、经验和灵感的环境，以帮助培养未来的领导者。

6：您如何在教学或设计实践中应用无障碍设计标准？

在过去的 30 年里，我设计的所有东西都力求在视觉上为目标观众所接受，包括 20/20 视力者、20/70 视力者、色盲色弱和阅读障碍者。视障、色盲和阅读障碍者占总人口的 19%。我使用优化方案来实现无障碍的视觉设计：1. 知道你设计的目标距离，这个原则经常被忽略；2. 测量对比度标准和距离的颜色；3. 测量字体的距离；4. 测量照片颜色对比度；5. 通过消除不必要的符号，运用照片/插图极简主义的原则；6. 为阅读障碍设置类型。这些就是信息无障碍视觉设计的"六大"原则。

在教授无障碍设计时，我们以这些原则为目标，并完全融入设计的制作过程中。我的两个最成功的案例是 APP 应用程序和用户工具包界面设计。这类项目范围很广，设计的每个方面都必须让视障、色盲色弱和阅读障碍者可以使用。学生开发的无障碍照片、插图、类型、颜色组合符合标准视障和色弱的观看距离，创建易于访问的图标，并为阅读障碍者设置更容易阅读的界面。学生需要彻底测试结果，并在制作原型之前以演示文稿的形式在多个反馈循环中展示信息，包括对应用程序或工具包进行竞争性审核，以确定 UI/UX 功能。

此外，用户价值的定义使用本尼森原则："1. 解决方案：产品与服务；2. 情境：场景和背景；3. 目标：人们想要达到的目标；4. 价值与意义：原因与原则；5. 功能性：必须具有功能性；6. 可靠：必须可靠；7. 可用：必须可用；8. 愉快/有意义：必须令人愉快。"正如本尼森所说："产品只有可用才对人们有意义。如果一个产品不可用，它就永远无法发挥其全部潜力。"可以确信，由于作业的复杂性，这对学生来说是一个非常具有挑战性的项目。但是，我发现该项目是让他们了解无障碍设计可视化实践的最快方式。

为了帮助学生完成无障碍设计作业，ICDE 有多个测试链接。链接列在主菜单的教育类别，而无障碍设计列在教育类菜单的首位。ICDE 有35个链接来帮助学生设计这些项目。此外，《ICDE：应用程序视觉无障碍白皮书》可以在 ICDE 网站上免费下载。

1: You recently published a white paper on Accessible Design. Can you talk about it? What is its intention and what changes do you expect it will bring to the design world?

The paper is entitled ICDE: White Paper for App Visual Accessibility, and Professors Sarah A. Meyer, Rene Bennyson, and I wrote the paper. The Innovation Center for Design Excellence (ICDE) recommends that individuals, educational associations, colleges and universities, organizations, and businesses embark on developing new tools, standards, and technology to make the world more accessible. To that end, this white paper lays out the information necessary to develop some of these tools and methods not only to promote new technology, but also to generate new educational standards to teach these methods, processes, and principles to others. The information contained in this paper can help 1.49 billion people with accessibility issues. ICDE hopes that this information will be the driving force not only for new technology, but also to update standards, legislation, software, fonts, and UI & UX toolkits, design templates, and more.

We now can scientifically predict the effects of distance, typographic form, color, and motion on visual acuity, comprising of not only 20/20 vision, but also all standardized eyesight, including the legally blind and visually impaired. We also include information on color, luminance values, Y tristimulus values, color contrast and how to measure it, fonts, font anatomy for maximizing viewing distance, measurements for calculating viewing distances for different visual acuities, tables for viewing distances of fonts (including their families), color vision deficiency (color-blindness) and how best to design for it, and scientific information for best practices when designing for those who have a reading disorder/dyslexia. Accessibility issues are a core value of ICDE's free education programming. ICDE believes that creating educational environments that are accessible to all individuals, no matter the impairment, is both achievable and necessary.

2: Accessible Design standards are made for people with disabilities and more general gives guidance for human centered design practices?

Accessible Design is a subset of Human Centered Design (HCD) and should not be confused with Universal Design, a subset all its own. Universal Design principles are used to create objects or environments that are accessible to all, for example, a sidewalk ramp or an automatic door that opens for anyone. Accessible Design specifically targets different types of disabilities and creates/develops new tools, standards, principles, and best design practices for an array of products that meet the type(s) of impairments, for example, iPhone apps. In the end, the product developed may be useful to all users and could certainly be classified as a universally designed product, but it has built into the design best practices for the intended users. Whereas HCD uses a methodology that puts the user first, developing empathy by studying the end user.

As explained by Professor Rene Bennyson, "For value to be created, the functionality of products must meet peoples' needs in four different ways.[1] 1) Products have to help or support what users are trying to achieve. 2) The function must be reliable for people to trust its purpose. 3) The function of the product must be usable in each situation. 4) For the value to be created, the operation of the product also must be pleasurable.[2] If the users' needs are not met in all four ways, the value of the product will not achieve its potential, and users will not find the product meaningful."

1, 2 Walter, Aarron. *Designing for Emotion*. A Book Apart/ Jeffrey Zeldman, 2011.

HCD methodology can certainly be used to help solve accessible design or universal design problems. In fact, HCD and accessible design tools and principles are most often used together to create a cogent agreement between the methodology used and the physicality of form in a series of feedback loops to produce the design and product.

3: Can you list some principles from Accessible Design standards?

First and foremost, communication design education around the world must start teaching 3-Dimensional Color Theory. Other design disciplines, product design, material design, architecture, and interior architecture know and use it, and for good reason. 3-Dimemsional Color Theory deals with the source (additive color theory), the object (subtractive color theory), and the observer. It is this third component that is missing in the educational process. Currently, the observer is the designer sitting in front of the computer, and this observer has no idea how to design for someone who has a type of impairment, nor do they understand the context of how the three (source, object, and observer) are different, where they match, and how they can work together to solve problems.

3-Dimensional Color Theory uses different types of color measurements, for example, Illuminance values and Tristimulus values, both of which measure the human response to color, in other words, how well human see color. In web design, Illuminance values are used to measure color contrast, and there are numerous sites (see links below[3]) that will measure and determine if the hues in question have enough color contrast to meet the visually impaired (20/70) vision. The color contrast for the visually impaired is defined by the Americans with Disabilities Act (ADA) and the World Wide Web Consortium (WC3).

To help determine the distance at which objects (type, icons, logos, or symbols) can be seen, the thinnest part of the object must be measured in points, be it the form or counter-form of the object. A one-point line in black and white has a viewing distance of 5 feet for 20/20 vision and 1.455 feet for 20/70 vision. In other words, a yellow-orange one- point line on a white background for 20/20 vision has a viewing distance of one foot, a loss of 80% of viewing distance. The same scenario with 20/70 vision would be .311, or roughly 4 inches of viewing distance. It is no wonder designers have a impossible time trying to design for the visually impaired because they have not been trained to do so.

When creating photos for the visually impaired, color contrast between objects must have a 40 CVD. To determine if the objects within a photo have the color contrast needed, use the Classic Digital Color meter to measure the objects, and objects and background (anything where one edge touches another). In other words, understanding the contrast needed between objects and backgrounds before taking a photograph is required. One must always think about how to position the objects within the shot prior to taking it. It is much easier to create the color contrast before taking the shot than it is to manipulate the photo after the fact. For the visually impaired, photo minimalism is the best approach.

Finally, know the target distance for the design you are creating. For example, an iPhone, iPad, magazines, and books all have a reading distance of 18 to 24 inches. For laptops, the distance is 30 inches, and for desk top computers, the working distance is from 33 to 36 inches.

---

3   https://toolness.github.io/accessible-color-matrix

4: From a strategic perspective, how does information design lead to brand innovation?

Edward Tufte said it best: "clutter and confusion are failures of design, not attributes of information." If a designer has the right information, then it will inherently inform and produce a better solution. The more you understand a subject, the more insight and innovation can be brought to bear. The days when designers, using their own God given talent, create a brand from their imagination are over. In fact, I don't think these days ever existed. Information design and its methods, processes, and practices help to visually frame research, making it easily understood by the user and/or client. Information design is a logical approach to understanding complex information, and to revealing patterns, characteristics, and facts to identify approaches. Information design can also be an approach to a solution. In other words, innovation comes from identifying the complex network and interconnected systems that make up a brand, and if done right, information design amplifies a brand ecosystem in an easily understood framwork.

5: Another focus of your personal research is design innovation, including the establishment of a non-profit creative center. What is its goal? How to booster creativity in the design community?

The Innovation Center for Design Excellence (ICDE)[4] is a 501(c)(3) nonprofit organization dedicated to fostering educational opportunities for underprivileged design students. ICDE will provide these students with scholarships, internships, and mentoring programs in partnership with our corporate sponsors, including professionals within the field. "According to the United States Census Report, Educational Attainment in the United States: 2015, only 32.5% of the United States population, 25 years and older, have a baccalaureate degree, and only 12% have an advanced degree (professional, master's, or doctorate)." This is simply not enough. Many of our most talented are being left behind. The Innovation Center for Design Excellence believes that many of the world's problems can be solved through education and opportunity. ICDE believes that creating educational environments that are accessible to all individuals, no matter the impairment, is both achievable and necessary, and through our free educational resources we train students to become accessible designers.

Through our website, ICDE provides free educational resources to anyone who shares a passion or need within the field of graphic and communication design. These educational resources are updated constantly through articles, lectures, tutorials, links, and postings that are vetted by board members, ambassadors, and educators within the field, and cover over 20 topics and/or subdisciplines within design.

In addition, ICDE sponsors national student design competitions to help these scholars gain recognition within the field. Currently ICDE runs over 10 national competitions, with plans to run more.

The Innovation Center for Design Excellence's vision is to be an agent of change and to provide life-altering opportunities for individuals who share a passion and need for design.

ICDE, is uniquely positioned to leverage the expertise of the design industry, educational community, diverse corporations in all fields, business partners, young talent, and individuals who share a passion and need for design, and is a place where these diverse

---

4   For more information, go to www.icde.co.

fields can come together. We provide the environment in which to create opportunities and to share ideas, experience, and inspiration to help educate tomorrow's leaders.

6: How do you apply Accessible Design standards in teaching and/or design practice?

For the past 30 years, everything I have designed has been visually accessible to the intended audience, including 20/20, 20/70 vision, color deficient (color blindness), and dyslexia. The visually impaired, color deficient, and dyslexics represent 19% of the total population, increasing the amount of end users who can participate in the designed experience. I use best practices for accessible design visualization; 1. Know the intended target distances of your design. This principle is quite often overlooked. 2. Measure color for both contrast standards and distance. 3. Measure the font(s) for distance. 4. Measure photo color contrast. 5. Use the principles of photo/illustration minimalism by eliminating unnecessary signifiers. 6. Set type for dyslexics. These are the "big six" principles for accessible design visualization.

When teaching accessible design, these best practices are used as the objective for assignments, and they are fully incorporated into the outcomes of the design. Two of the most successful projects are a prototype app or a user interface toolkit. These projects are extensive, and every aspect of the design must be accessible to the visually impaired, color deficient, and dyslexic. Students develop accessible photos and/or illustrations and type and color combinations that meet standards and viewing distances for the visually impaired and color deficient, create icons that are accessible, and set type for dyslexics that is easier to read. The students are required to thoroughly test outcomes, and present the information in multiple feedback loops in the form of a presentation deck

before prototyping, including a competitive audit of apps or toolkits to determine both the UI and UX functionality. In addition, user values are defined using Rene Bennyson's principles: "1. Solutions: products and services, 2. Situations: Scenarios and context, 3. Goals: What people want to achieve, 4. Values and Meanings: Reasons and principles, 5. Functional: Must be functional, 6. Reliable: Must be reliable, 7. Usable: Must be usable, and 8. Pleasurable/Meaningful: Must be pleasurable." As Bennyson states, "Products need to be useable to become meaningful to people. If a product is not usable, it will never reach its full potential." To be sure, this is a very challenging project for students due to the complexity of the assignment. However, I have found the project to be the fastest way to get them up to speed on accessible design visualization best practices.

To assist students in accessible assignments, ICDE has multiple testing links. The links are listed under education in the main menu, and accessible design is listed first in this menu. In addition, ICDE: White Paper for App Visual Accessibility is a free downloadable on the ICDE website.

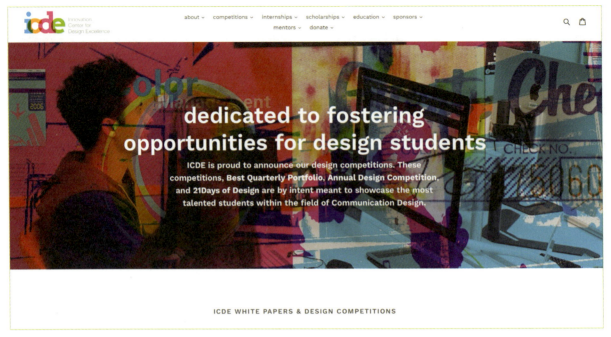

图1 ICDE网站（www.icde.co）

图2 《色彩管理：色彩设计的统筹与应用》一书被翻译为多国文字出版

design education in progress

application process

Design Education in Process is a program that continues a tradition of publishing articles on the subject of design education. This journal series was first published by the Center for Design Studies, Communication Arts + Design, Virginia Commonwealth University, and is an in-depth resource for design education. This program hopes to fill some of the needs within the field by exploring topics in depth. Design Education in Progress provides a broad collection of in-depth resources that explore one topic at a time, and it is an economical resource that provokes awareness, communicates methodology, and advocates process to all interested parties no matter how isolated they may be. All articles are peer-reviewed within communication design.

Search

图3 ICDE网站（www.icde.co）

ICDE WHITE PAPERS & DESIGN COMPETITIONS

Free ICDE White Paper
$0.00

Poster Design Competition
Deadline Date 01.26.2022
$10.00

Logo Design Competition
Deadline Date 2.05.2022
$10.00

Package Design Competition
Deadline Date: 3/15/2022
$10.00

Branding Competition
Deadline Date: 4.1.2022
$10.00

Book Cover Competition
Deadline Date 4.01.2022
$10.00

Motion Graphics Deadline
Date: 3.31.2022
$10.00

Book and Magazine Design
Deadline Date: 12.10.2021
$10.00

图4 ICDE网站（www.icde.co）

FXKE (2021)

JIAYUN ZHUANG
庄稼昀

KEYWORDS:
Storytelling, p|Public spaces, Theaters and Social scenes
故事叙述，公共空间，剧场与社会场景

1：作为一名戏剧工作者，您一直非常强调剧本的思辨性。这仍然是您最近工作的重点吗？

我作为独立戏剧工作者的剧场实践，与我在保留剧目剧场中的戏剧实践不太一样。和其他独立戏剧工作者一样，我们的创作会有意识地在主流戏剧传统之外进行探索，比如寻找新的美学形式、叙事观念、观演关系、技术手段、甚至是戏剧活动组织和生产方式的可能性等。在这种语境下，我的角色一般来说是文本/作者，若细分，有时候是策划，有时候是剧构，偶尔也被称为编剧。

在今天经常被标记为"后戏剧/展演导向"的戏剧生态中，戏剧和展演的边界模糊，文本的功能面临着史无前例的挑战，也获得了创新的无限可能。比如说，演出依附于文本（这里的文本特指那些以清晰的叙事结构和目的论作为特征的文学剧本）的传统等级秩序被逐渐打破。文本，即使它仍然存在和发生，也将和其他戏剧参数进行平等开放、更加刺激的游戏，而并非掌控全局。

我以编舞克里斯朵·派特和文本乔纳森·杨共同创作的舞蹈剧场*Revisor*（2020）作个例子。[1]这部戏剧衍生自果戈里1836年的五幕讽刺喜剧《钦差大臣》的标准戏剧文学剧本。[2]作品起始，全知视角的画外音开场，以剧本为纲指挥全场。舞者们在服装、化妆、道具、景片中手舞足蹈，唇舞着他们事先录制的人物台词，将夸张的动作和录音中的台词节奏对齐，由此展现果戈理笔下小官僚系统里的平庸，以及身份错误类喜剧中的各式鸡毛蒜皮。后半场转而切题，好似所有戏剧元素化身为"Revisor"，进入了不断修正的状态。预先录制的台词终止播放，布景道具清空。空舞台上，舞者们以中性装扮一次次修改编舞细节，营造出一种流畅、梦幻和脆

1　我是在2020年3月11日于阿姆斯特丹城市剧院看到的这个作品。更多信息可见官网https://kiddpivot.org/works/revisor/ 。

2　乔纳森·杨将 Revizor 更改为 Revisor，也就是负责编辑、重写、修改的人，特别是负责法律文本的语言结构、转换文本格式以供出版。

弱的现代舞氛围。为了营造解构氛围，音乐灯光也更加抽象。"作者"的声音时断时续、破碎不堪。文本现在和作品的编舞、视觉、音乐等元素合作和竞争。所有这些戏剧成分重建着新的展演文本，一边创建、一边修订。

*Revisor*虽说有些说教味道，也没有超越传统的观演框架，但是它生动地诠释了展演文本如何从文学文本中解放出来。我在戏剧领域的工作属性正经历着类似的变化。今天，我仍然为演出提供书面形式的文本材料，但我的首要任务不再是完成演出需遵循的"一剧之本"。我设计作品的框架、语境、游戏规则、甚至技术脚本。在确定总体方向后，我和其他艺术家合作设计一系列戏剧符号：视觉的、时空的、编排的、即兴的，等等。随着创作向制作和演出的进一步发展，我们继续实验诸戏剧元素之间关系模式的变化可能。

2: 剧场是一个交叉学科的合作环境。您与您的团队如何分工合作？如果出现意见分歧，作为编剧，您如何来协调各个部分的关系？

我还是就后戏剧/展演导向的戏剧工作语境来回答这个问题。一般来说，作为作者，我在策划阶段与导演、编舞或其他媒介艺术家合作，构思作品的框架、结构、媒介互文可能等。策划阶段集思广益，出现意见分歧再正常不过。对我来说，更重要的是以作品的终极目标为基础来思考如何应用和表达主创构思中的分歧（或汇集），并且判断目标受众的感知系统和能动性。例如，我们都知道不同的媒介以不同的属性来塑造信息，并以不同的方式接触观众。一味地做加法，特别是随便添加不同媒介的材料，或许会导致作品中的符号材料过多，各说各话。那么这个时候，我就需要判断几个关键因素：信息密度和符号转化有效性、作品的清晰度、观众预期的互动程度、信息的过载或匮乏如何影响观众创造性参与，等等。

作为在排练阶段中主导创作和编作的文本/作者，我也负责构作最适合该过程的戏剧方法：我可能会设计有针对性的工作坊，对排练中发展出来的有效片段进行整合编撰，并最后完成一个相对完整的演出文本。担任剧构的时候，我为团队提供关于文化、社会、历史、心理等

方面的参考资料。剧构"如镜子般映照TA所看到的"，[3]那么我带着新鲜的眼光进入排练，成为反思作品的第一批观众，通过向导演/编舞给予反馈、提出问题、提供选择，而给予具有批判性的、中立的支持，并最终为整个作品提供支持。

3: 在信息设计过程中，内容的组织是叙述的安排，信息的传递是讲故事。那么，如何定义一个好故事呢？ 它需要具备哪些特点？

和诸多其他创意领域一样，今天的戏剧不仅要讲故事(storytelling)，也要发展"活在故事中"(storyliving)。也就是说，融合情节和行动，策划特定的、具身的体验，将观众置于体验核心。[4]从某种程度上，这个发展其实是戏剧展演领域在面对沉浸在各种视觉和多媒体资源中的新观众时，需要思考的创作策略。传统戏剧观众习惯以镜框作为自己与舞台叙事之间的边界。在新媒体实践中，很大一部分观众很有可能从一开始已将自我定位和主体想象延伸进了镜框/屏幕中，并对场景体验和参与表达出了更强烈的渴望。由此，来自不同领域的设计师、艺术家、研究者都在探索观众如何切身、即时、主动地生活在故事中，以及如何通过这种体验扩展他们的视角、唤醒新的叙事可能，并加深他们的同情同理。英国Punchdrunk剧团的沉浸式剧场《无人入眠》的巨大成功，和由此开启的沉浸式产业的蓬勃发展，都表明了如果呼应新的视听体验和叙事需要，戏剧可预见的未来之一便是将"活在故事中"物理化、实体化。

但同时我也在思考，倘若我们把戏剧界定放宽，特别是将展演（展演性）纳入考量，那么除了"活在故事"当中，还能如何"把故事讲好"？此外，什么又有资格成为故事？这里我想借用戏剧理论家博特·斯戴特的观点来讨论戏剧媒介的特殊性："戏剧[……]以最真实的形式消耗真实：人、他的语言、他的房间和城市、他的武器和工具、他的其他艺术、动物、火和水，甚至戏剧

3　参考由Hildegard De Vuyst等人编写的，探索比利时著名编舞Alain Platel作品的The Choreopolitics of Alain Platel's les ballets C de la B, Bloomsbury 出版社2020年出版，引文见51页。

4　2017年，谷歌新闻实验室在研究沉浸式新闻的文章中，从人类学研究中提炼出"活在故事中"这个概念，提出观众/用户要体验故事而不是听故事。https://newslab.withgoogle.com/assets/docs/storyliving-a-study-of-vr-in-journalism.pdf

本身。"[5] 在这个论述中，正因为戏剧可以利用日常生活中的方方面面作为原材料，真实与幻象由此不仅可以在多个维度上并列，而且还可以被交叉共享；它们的边界愈发模糊。由此，戏剧观众可以运用双目视觉的感知能力：他们以符号学的方式阅读一切，所以一个意义总被传至下一个意义；他们又以现象学的方式感受，所以一切都只有它的本身。[6]

今年早些时候我们在格里菲斯公园体验过的艾伦·瑞德声音漫步可以作为一个有点极端的例子。[7] 当我们将自己视为瑞德作品的观众时，声音漫步便围绕我们发展：我们戴上耳机在公园中漫步，将自己沉浸在精心创作的声音和音乐中；我们允许GPS服务通过手机上的应用程序跟踪我们的路径、并将每个声音/音乐片段与我们的特定位置进行匹配；我们感受自然景观和人造声场之间的融合与张力，也不时地测试着应用程序的功能性、可靠性和原创性。与此同时，我们还可以在同一个时空现实中轻而易举地脱离这个展演框架——特别是艾伦·瑞德声音漫步的框架本身就是相当非叙事、非模仿的。而在这种脱离中，我们也成为非符号的。这类展演作品的讲故事技巧在"生活"中点出"故事"，在"故事"中浮现"生活"，由此参与者可以占据或徘徊在符号编码和现象学视角之间。我想，戏剧可以奉献的最独特的讲故事（和信息设计）的方法，正如艾伦·瑞德声音漫步的预期目标一样，短暂而偶然地存在于日常与戏剧的混杂中。它不断激发我们的感知机制和认知想象，无论我们是观众还是日常生活的一员：徒步旅行者、音乐爱好者、应用程序发烧用户，等等。（见图7-9）

5　见博特·斯戴特1985年的关于戏剧现象学的著作：*Great Reckonings in Little Rooms: On the Phenomenology of Theater*，加州大学出版社出版，引文见第40页。

6　引文见第8页。斯戴特写道："If we think of semiotics and phenomenology as modes of seeing, we might say that they constitute a kind of binocular vision: one eye enables us to see the world phenomenally; the other eye enables us to see it significatively [...] Lose the sight of your phenomenal eye and you become a Don Quixote (everything is something else); lose the sight of your significative eye and you become Sartre's Roquentin (everything is nothing but itself)."

7　我和王琛教授于 2021 年 9 月 1 日体验了艾伦·瑞德声音漫步。三个月后，即 2021 年 12 月 1 日，我再次体验这个作品。这次我选择了不同的路线，并关闭了移动数据。关于这个作品的更多介绍，请访问 https://www.ellenreidsoundwalk.com/ 。

4: 您在剧场空间中使用了什么样的互动方式？在我们以前的交流中您已提到一些，比如内容交互、介面交互、媒介交互、人机交互、观众与作者身份交互等，能具体讲讲吗？

我和不同的团队做过几种互动尝试。这里我先举两个在传统剧场空间中实验的例子。在三种碗创作的舞蹈剧场《流量》中，我们叠加了具有不同展演特征的两种媒介：戏剧和直播。在作品中，表演者在舞台上做直播，同时参与两组展演机制和观演关系。戏剧观众和他们的现场互动成为直播素材，而直播观众的反馈反过来又刺激了现场行动。广义上来说，两套媒介都具有交互传播的特性，并产生实时反馈。然而，作为一种流行社交网络实践，直播很大程度上已被直播平台货币化，成为致力于制作流量驱动内容和制造互动营销的媒介。因此，《流量》的部分戏剧张力来自于两种观演互动模式，特别是它们就亲密性和即时性的不同诱导方式对表演者-主播所造成的迷惑和疲惫。这个作品也尝试在戏剧和直播两种媒介间建构了跨媒介关系。更具体地说，作为一个剧场作品，《流量》用剧场这套媒介来再现了直播媒介，也以剧场的方式来触摸直播。如果我们从直播的角度来再现戏剧呢？这个问题为我们未来的相关作品提供了一个创意。

另一个具有互动元素的戏剧作品是与新青年剧团合作的《美好的一天》(2013)。这个作品自2013年在北京首演后，持续在中国的不同城市制作和上演。每次演出都会招募将近20位在当地的非职业表演者。他们受邀在舞台上坐成一排，同时讲述他们与这座城市有关的故事。招募团队特意寻找表演者在职业、年龄、文化程度、出身地区、家庭构成等特征上的差异。在现场，每位表演者携带一个发射器，产生一个特定的无线频道。观众进场时会拿到一副耳机、一个接收器，以及一本写有每位表演者小传的手册。在接下来大约75分钟左右的演出时间中，观众可随时切换频道，决定如何收听表演者的故事。表演者没有专业技艺、不具备所谓的主角权威、也没有可以博得观众青睐的舞台景观；但观众的主动选择也几乎不会对现场有任何影响。事实上，这个作品旨在建立一种心理上的互动模式。在有限时间框架和过剩叙事材料的前提下，因为观演互动的不可能，剧目在观众那里产生了最大限度的提高互动性的需求。根据每场演后谈，我们了解到观演各方都竭尽全力地促进信息传递，即使他们预料其结果仍然不可避免地受到限制。一方面表演者不断诉说，而越说则越为场上的众声喧哗添加噪音；另一方面观众尽可能地倾听和辨别，但是他们切换频道越频繁，信息就越碎片化。

5: 您认为AR/VA是一种技术辅助手段，还是一种更本质的语言叙述手段？

对我来说，通过戏剧与增强现实（AR）和虚拟现实（VR）技术的结合，可以有效诱发观众的阈限意识状态。在人类学和展演研究学者维克多·特纳的理论中，阈限是一个非此非彼、模棱两可的状态，是明确和接受的界限之外的门槛阶段，[8] 可以通过仪式实现。也许AR和VR技术可以被视作进入阈限的现代仪式（手段），但是同样重要的是看到这股神奇的力量源于数字技术和戏剧的共同努力。也就是说，虽然AR和VR技术有助于将观众沉浸在计算机生成的现实中，但戏剧的本体特征之一是对物理性和具身化的永恒要求。正是这两者的结合激发了阈限摩擦，使人"感觉被沉浸式的空间裹着、被虚拟世界的他者感奇怪地影响着[……]既没有完全迷失、也没有完全沉浸在体验中"。[9] 当AR与VR技术沉浸（个体）观众的视听体验时，戏剧可以通过其技术特点切入观众的其他感官功能，如嗅觉、味觉、触觉、动觉，甚至可以调动观众作为一个群体可以共享甚至共创的现场性。AR/VR戏剧可以利用数字信息与物理世界的叠加、熟悉界与新奇界的叠加触发观众的门槛状态，开启他们的过渡机制。这是观众借助他们的地域化记忆、具身化的想象，以敬畏、脆弱、开放的姿态，进入给定的多维时空。我想从这个角度上来说，AR/VR不仅仅是技术，也是认识论：我们用AR/VR重新感知时间、空间、身份和意识，而AR/VR塑造我们的所知，也提供了关于我们的更多可能。

6: 能分享一些你最近项目的细节吗？

我最近策划并参与的作品名为FXKE(2021)，这是个在非常规剧场空间里体验的作品。这个作品切入"眼球货币化"的注意力经济，特别是从这种经济中衍生出的后真相数字环境以及它对社会认知安全的挑战。FXKE有两个目标：一是在实体展演空间中模拟数字社交媒体环境，通过信息过载和屏幕过载刺激观众的行动；二是将数字媒体环境不设防的、无人监管的生成能量导入作品中，将观众的参与（无论主动参与还是被动参与）转化为实时的、基于算法的、奖励驱动的内容生成机制的原材料。更具体来说，观众的照片将成为作品视觉生成的素材；观众需随时使用手机访问作品的网站、与聊天机器人进行交流，由此他们的言论将被带入作品的叙事生成；[10] 他们还被邀请在作品中进行几轮投票，以决定生成工具如何运行、生成演出文本的下一部分。我们刚刚在德国多特蒙德市的戏剧和数字学院完成了作品第一个阶段的研究、制作和展示。在下一阶段中，我们计划进一步强化作品的生成特性，这将涉及获取更多的观众数据（如：声音、动作、体温以及他们选择上传的信息），并将其转化为演出材料。人工智能生成的内容也将经过演员的即兴发挥而继续发酵。简而言之，FXKE希望让观众以一个实体群体参与到人与人工智能在数字化信息内容生成方面的"合谋"中去，并体验这种合谋对真相基础近乎偏执的破坏。

---

8 见维克多·特纳1967年出版人类学著作 *The Forest of Symbols: Aspects of Ndembu Ritual*。康奈尔大学出版社1967年出版。关于阈限的论述主要来自于第四章"Betwixt and Between: The Liminal Period in Rites de Passage"。

9 见罗斯·比金2017年关于沉浸式戏剧的著作：*Immersive Theatre and Audience Experience Space, Game and Story in the Work of Punchdrunk*，Palgrave Macmillan出版社出版，引文见第21页。同时可参考上述引文的出处：艾莉森·格里菲斯2008年的关于沉浸式观看的著作：*Shivers Down Your Spine: Cinema, Museums and the Immersive View*，哥伦比亚大学出版社出版，引文见第3页。

10 作品的网站为 http://thefxke.com/。无论就功能还是内容而言，这个网站都是现场演出的内在组成部分。网站的绝大部分内容由GPT-3生成。GPT-3 是OpenAI开发的一种语言预测模型：它被训练来学习字符的概率分布，在模仿人类语言的能力上比以往任何语言模型都更加令人信服。

My practice in the independent theatre scene is quite different from what it would be in a conventional, repertory setting. My work, like that of my fellow practitioners in independent theatre-making, deliberately explores something beyond mainstream theatre conventions. We investigate new possibilities in terms of aesthetics, narrative concepts, spectatorial expanses, technical applications, and even organizational and production models. In this context, my role is generally defined as "writer"—more specifically, sometimes I am called a concept developer, sometimes a dramaturg, and, occasionally, a playwright.

Theatre today claims to be freed from the hierarchical primacy of the literary text (script), particularly the kind of literal script characterized by unified narrative structure and teleology. Now is the time for that piece of text, if it still exists, to interact with all the other theatrical parameters on an equal basis instead of continuing to govern the entire theatrical proceeding.

Revisor (2020), a co-creation between choreographer Crystal Pite and writer Jonathon Young, provides a good example.[1] This dance theatre piece is derived from Nikolai Gogol's five-act satirical play *The Inspector General* (Revizor in Russian).[2] Originally published in 1836, it is a typical piece of dramatic literature. In the first half of Pite and Young's Revisor, a female voice is heard dictating the staging of the literary text. Costumed performers, as various characters surrounded by sets and props, lip-synch to scripted, previously recorded, disembodied voiceovers (of their lines) and align their exaggerated movements to the stop-start rhythm of those words. These techniques all enhance Gogol's treatment of both the banality of petty bureaucracy and the triviality of a classical mistaken identity comedy. In the second half, echoing the title, each theatrical component of Revisor starts to work loose from the original storyline and to undergo a process of change. The pre-recorded voiceovers stop; sets and props clear out. Now in nondescript costumes and on an empty stage, the performers revise their previous movements to create an ambiance of fluid, dreamlike, and vulnerable modern dance. Lights and music become more abstract, serving the deconstructive twist. The final tones of the "authorial" voice turn staccato and ragged; its jobs now are to both collaborate and compete with the choreographic, the visual, and the musical of the production. Together, all of these theatrical components create a performance text that lends itself well to constant and simultaneous revisions.

Despite being slightly too didactic and not venturing beyond the proscenium frame, Revisor vividly plays with the concept of emancipating the performance text from the literary text. The nature of my role in theatre and performance has undergone similar changes. Today, I still provide written forms of material for a performance. However, my priority is no longer to create (spoken) text that functions, in its finished form, as the base for a representation of a reality. Instead, I create the framework, context, parameters, and even technical scripts for the given work. Next, after this general direction is set, I collaborate with other artists to design the visual, the temporospatial, the choreographic, the improvisational, and so forth. As the creative process then unfolds toward perfor-

---

1   I saw the production of Revisor at the Stadsschouwburg of Amsterdam on March 11, 2020. For more information of the piece, visit https://kiddpivot.org/works/revisor/.

2   Young changes Revizor into Revisor: someone who is responsible for the linguistic construction of texts, particularly legal texts, and puts them into the appropriate formats for publication. This description, as we can imagine, applies to someone whose job is to redact, rewrite, revise, etc.

mance, we continue to experiment the dramaturgical composition in ways that provide dynamism for modes of relationship among all these theatrical elements.

2: Theatre is an interdisciplinary collaborative environment. How do you and your team work together? As a theatre-maker, how do you coordinate the relationship between the various parts if there are differences in opinion?

Again, I will approach the question from the context of working in the postdramatic, performance-oriented theatre ecology. Generally speaking, in the conceptual phase, as a writer, I work together with the director/choreographer and artists in other mediums, to plan out the framework, structure, and interactive/intertextual potentials of the piece. Divergence of views is most commonly encountered in this stage, which is essentially a process of brainstorming. It is critical for me to think during this planning phase about how to apply and express such divergence (or convergence) based on the ultimate goal of the work. It is also essential for me to consider the perceptual apparatus and activity of the intended audience. For example, we know that different mediums have different attributes that shape messages, and reach audiences in different ways. Simply adding content, particularly content with different medium characteristics, may lead to an overabundance of symbolic material, and each material fragment simply utters its own note. Therefore, I must estimate several crucial factors: information density and the efficacy of conversion of signs, the definition level of each participating medium, the projected interactive level of the audience, and the ways plethora or deprivation of signs influence the creative engagement of the audience.

As the writer who leads the process of creating and devising during the rehearsal period, I am also responsible for developing the dramaturgy, which is best suited to that process. In service of this responsibility, I may design workshops with targeted goals, curate collages selected from the rehearsals, and compose/deliver a relatively complete text. When working as a dramaturg, I compile cultural, social, historical, psychological, and other references for the rest of the creative team. In addition, because "a dramaturg is a mirror that reflects what you see,"[3] I attend rehearsals with fresh eyes and function as a reflective first audience. I critically and neutrally reflect what I see, and support the director, the choreographer, et al. with feedback, questions, and strategies. By doing so, I ultimately support the production as a whole.

3: In the process of information design, the organization of content is the arrangement of narration, and the delivery of information refers to storytelling. So, how do you define a good story? What characteristics does it need?

As with many other creative fields, theatre today not only tells a story but also lives it. The newly coined term, "storyliving," fuses plot and action, orchestrates specific lived and embodied experiences, and places the audience at the heart of those experiences.[4] To some extent, this development can be understood as a needed creative strategy, as theatre is facing new audiences that have grown up immersed in various new visual and multimedia resources. Traditional audiences in conventional theatre are used to a proscenium, which functions as the boundary that separates them from the staged storytelling.

---

3   See *The Choreopolitics of Alain Platel's les ballets C de la B*, Bloomsbury Publishing, 2020, page 51.

4   Deriving from "anthropological research on the concept of the lived story," Google News Lab's 2017 study of VR in journalism proposed storyliving as describing the idea that audience/users are "living the story as opposed to being told it". https://newslab.withgoogle.com/assets/docs/storyliving-a-study-of-vr-in-journalism.pdf

In the new media practices, a significant portion of audiences have probably already extended their self-positioning and imagination of subjectivity beyond this screen, and harbor a more pronounced desire for a heightened sense of mise-en-scène and engagement. Accordingly, designers, artists, and researchers in several fields have explored how audiences live a story viscerally, immediately, and actively, as well as how audiences, through such experiences, expand their perspectives, awaken new narrative possibilities, and deepen their own senses of emotional engagement and empathy. For example, the enormous success of Punchdrunk's production of Sleep No More and the subsequent rapid evolution of the immersive industry indicate that, if theatre is to respond to the audiovisual and narrative demands of these new audiences, one of its foreseeable futures lies in the type of physical embodiment demonstrated by storyliving.

Meanwhile, I have also been wondering: If we expand the boundaries of theatre to specifically include performance (and performativity), what besides storyliving will make a good story? Moreover, what would even qualify as a story? I refer here to performance studies theorist Bert States' thoughts on the unique characteristics of theatre as a medium that "consumes the real in its realest forms: man, his language, his rooms and cities, his weapons and tools, his other arts, animals, fire, and water-even, finally, theater itself."[5] In States' theorization, because theatre can utilize every aspect of everyday life as raw material, the real and the illusionary, in multiple dimensions, can be not only juxtaposed but also intersected and shared. Their distinctions are increasingly becoming murky. Thus, for its part, the theatre audience can operate with is perceptual "binocular vision"; that is, they can perceive everything significatively, so everything is something else, while at the same time they also can perceive everything phenomenally, so everything is nothing but itself.[6]

An extreme example would be Ellen Reid SOUNDWALK, which we experienced in LA's Griffith Park earlier this year.[7] When we in attendance take ourselves as the audience of Reid's composition and design, the soundwalk project evolves and revolves around us. We immerse ourselves in the deliberately composed sound and music through headphones while wandering around in this large municipal park. We let GPS services through an app track our path and match each sound and music piece to the specific location we are at. We experience the blend and tension between the natural landscape and the created soundscape. As we do all these things, we also test the versatility, reliability, and originality of the app. Yet, at the same time, we can easily break from this performative frame even if we remain in the same temporal and spatial reality, especially as the frame of SOUNDWALK is rather non-narrative and non-mimetic to begin with. Consequently, if we perform this break, doing so turns us into something non-semiotic. Because the "storytelling technique" of this kind of theatre and performance work, such as it is, spots "the story" within "living," and vice versa, audience engagement consists of occupying and wandering through a literal and figurative space between semiotic coding and phenomenological perspective. I believe the most unique storytelling

5   See Bert O. States' *Great Reckonings in Little Rooms: On the Phenomenology of Theater*, page 40.

6   See States, page 8. He writes, "If we think of semiotics and phenomenology as modes of seeing, we might say that they constitute a kind of binocular vision: one eye enables us to see the world phenomenally; the other eye enables us to see it significantly [...] Lose the sight of your phenomenal eye and you become a Don Quixote (everything is something else); lose the sight of your significative eye and you become Sartre's Roquentin (everything is nothing but itself)..."

7   I experienced the soundwalk on September 1, 2021, with my friend Professor Wang Shen. Three months later, on December 1, 2021, I experienced the soundwalk again, on a different route and with the mobile data turned off. For more information about the Soundwalk, visit https://www.ellenreid-soundwalk.com/.

and information design method that theatre can offer, as per the intended goals of Ellen Reid SOUNDWALK, exists ephemerally and contingently in the "doubling" between everyday life and the performative, which constantly catalyzes the perceptual mechanisms and cognitive imaginations we hold as audience members who are also, in our way, members of daily life (hikers, music-lovers, app aficionados, etc.).

4: Your team has also been paying attention to interactions in theatre. What kind of interactive methods have you used in the theatre space?

I have tried a few forms of interaction in theatre and performance with different teams. First let me give two examples of the experiments conducted in conventional theatre spaces. In Web Traffic (2018), a dance-theatre piece created by The Three Bowls Co-op, we blend two mediums that have different performative characteristics: theatre and livestreaming. In one section of the piece, the performer livestreams from the stage, simultaneously engaging two sets of performance mechanism and spectatorial relation. The theatre audience and their live interactions are turned into broadcast material, and the feedback from the livestreaming viewers, in turn, stimulates onstage actions. Broadly speaking, both mediums have interactive communication characteristics and generate real-time feedback. However, as a popular social-networking practice extensively monetized by dedicated platforms, livestreaming has moved closer to producing traffic-driven content and geared more toward interactive marketing. Therefore, part of the dramatic tension of Web Traffic comes from the ways that the two modes of performer-audience interaction, especially in terms of how differently they induce intimacy and immediacy, confuse and even deplete the performer-streamer. Web Traffic also builds an intermedial relationship between the two mediums of theatre and livestreaming. More specifically, as a piece that

is essentially theatre, Web Traffic represents the medium of livestreaming via a theatrical representation system; thus it approaches livestreaming from the perspective of theatre. The question of what a piece might look like if we were to represent theatre from the anchor point of livestreaming supplies a creative idea for future work.

Another theatre piece with interactive components is One Fine Day (2013) by The New Youth Group. It premiered in 2013 and has continued to stage in different cities in China. In each place, nearly 20 non-professional local people are recruited for the performance. They are invited to sit on stage, in a row, and simultaneously share their stories about the city. The recruiting team deliberately looks for performers who demonstrate a range of occupations, ages, education levels, areas of origin, family compositions, and other characteristics. In the performance, each performer carries a transmitter that generates a specific radio channel. When the audience members enter the venue, each is given earphones, a receiver, and a handbook that includes each performer's biography. During the performance, which lasts approximately 75 minutes, the audience switches channels and decides how to listen to the stories. While the performers have no professional virtuosity, no so-called lead actor's authority, and nothing much resembling a staged spectacle with which to win favor from the audience, the audience's active choices also rarely impact the staging. In fact, One Fine Day intends to establish a mode of interaction that is essentially psychological. Under premises that include a limited time frame and an excess of narrative material, the impossibility of performer-audience interaction creates a need within the audience to maximize interactivity. We learned during the post-show discussions after each performance that many participants in One Fine Day had done their best to facilitate the transmission of information, despite their understanding that the results would be inevitably limited. On the one hand, the performers keep talking; yet the more they utter, the more noise they contribute to the cacophonic staging. On the other hand, audience members try to listen and discern as much as possible; yet the more frequently they switch channels, the more fragmented the information becomes.

5: Do you think VA and AR are a kind of assistive technology means, or a more essential language narrative means?

In my practical experience of applying augmented reality (AR) and virtual reality (VR) technologies to theatrical performance, it is possible to induce a liminal state of consciousness. To put it simply, as per anthropologist and performance scholar Victor Turner's theorization, liminality is the condition of "betwixt and between."[8] As the threshold phase among well-delineated, accepted boundaries, it can be achieved via ritual practices. To this end, AR and VR technologies can be seen as modern-day rites of passage for entry into liminal states; however, it is also important to acknowledge that the power behind such magic resides in collaborative efforts between digital technologies and theatre. It is true that AR and VR technologies help immerse the audience in computer-generated reality. But one of the ontological characteristics of theatre begs the eternal request for physicality and embodiment. The resulting combination stimulates a liminal friction, so that one "feels enveloped in immersive spaces and strangely affected by a strong sense of the otherness of the virtual world [...] neither fully lost in the experience nor completely in the here and now."[9] Whereas AR and VR technologies engage the visual and auditory senses of the audience as a collection of individuals, theatre can probe the other sensory faculties (e.g., smell, taste, touch, kinesthesis) and mobilize the audience as a community to share and even co-create liveness. AR/VR theatre-makers can take advantage of such superpositions of digital information and the physical world, as well as of both the familiar and the novel, to trigger the audience's threshold phase and switch on their mechanisms of transition. This is when the audience may inhabit the given multidimensional surrounding environments by using their localized memories and embodied imaginations, in states that range through awe, vulnerability, and openness. From this perspective, AR/VR is not only technology but also epistemology: we use AR/VR to restructure our time, space, identity, and consciousness. As we do so, it not only shapes what we know but also points to the possibilities of who we can be.

6: Can you share some examples and images of your recent projects? Thank you.

The work I have conceptualized and participated in most recently, titled FXKE (2021), is a performance meant to be experienced in an unconventional theatre space. It looks at today's eyeball-monetized attention economy, from which a post-truth digital environment has derived and challenged a society's epistemic security. FXKE has two goals. One is to simulate the digital social media experience in the physical theatrical space and thereby to stimulate the audience's actions via information and screen overload. The second is to channel the unguarded and unsupervised generative energy of the digital media environment into the performance, and thereby to turn the audience's participations, be it active or passive, into raw material for the real-time, algorithm-based, reward-driven content generation

8   See Victor Turner's "Betwixt and Between: The Liminal Period in Rites of Passage," in Turner, *The Forest of Symbols: Aspects of Ndembu Ritual* (Ithaca, 1967), 93– 111. Betwixt and Between: The Liminal Period in Rites de Passage

9   *Immersive Theatre and Audience Experience Space, Game and Story in the Work of Punchdrunk.* Page 21.

mechanism. More specifically: Photos of the audience are taken as the base for visual generation of the performance; audiences are required to use their mobile phones to visit the FXKE website, where they interact with a chatbot and thereby bring their words into the generation of performance narrative.[10] They are also invited to poll a few times during the performance, so their decisions determine how the generative tools operate to produce the next section of the performance text. We have just completed the first stage of research, production, and presentation of FXKE at the Academy for Theatre and Digitality in Germany. In the next stage, we plan to further intensify the piece's generative characteristics. This will involve obtaining more audience data (e.g., voices, movements, body temperatures, along with the other information they choose to upload) and folding it into the performance. The AI-generated content will also be performed and altered through real performers' improvisations. In short, FXKE expects the audience, as an embodied community, to participate in the "collusion" between humans and AIs in terms of content generation, and to experience through the performance a compulsive undermining of the accepted infrastructure of truth.

---

10   The website, http://thefxke.com/, is an intrinsic part of the live performance in terms of both function and content. Most of the website content is generated by GPT-3, an ai-powered language prediction model developed by OpenAI. It has been trained to learn a probability distribution over tokens and imitate human language more convincingly than any previous language model.

图1-4 FXKE (2021)

图5 FXKE (2021)

图6 演出现场

图7 用户手机屏幕截图，艾伦·瑞德声音
漫步 https://www.ellenreidsoundwalk.com

图书在版编目（ＣＩＰ）数据

信息设计与品牌塑造 / 闵洁, 王琛编著. -- 上海：
上海文化出版社, 2024.2
ISBN 978-7-5535-2732-1

Ⅰ. ①信… Ⅱ. ①闵… ②王… Ⅲ. ①品牌战略
Ⅳ. ①F273.2

中国国家版本馆CIP数据核字(2023)第113408号

INFORMATION DESIGN
& BRANDING
信息设计与品牌塑造

出 版 人：姜逸青
责任编辑：罗　英 张悦阳
装帧设计：王　琛

书　　　名：信息设计与品牌塑造
编　　　著：闵洁 王琛
出　　　版：上海世纪出版集团　上海文化出版社
地　　　址：上海市闵行区号景路159弄A座3楼　201101
发　　　行：上海文艺出版社发行中心
　　　　　　上海市闵行区号景路159弄A座2楼206室　201101　www.ewen.co
印　　　刷：上海界龙艺术印刷有限公司
开　　　本：787 × 1092　1/16
印　　　张：12
印　　　次：2024年2月第一版　2024年2月第一次印刷
书　　　号：ISBN 978-7-5535-2732-1/J.615
定　　　价：108.00元
告 读 者：如发现本书有质量问题请与印刷厂质量科联系 021-58925888